BE TRUE & SERVE

AUTOBIOGRAPHY

DOROTHEA GUTZEIT

with Irene Riznek (Koenigsberger)

DOROTHEA GUTZEIT

BE
TRUE
& SERVE

AUTOBIOGRAPHY

Library and Archives Canada Cataloguing in Publication
Gutzeit, Dorothea, 1921-2005, author
Be true & serve : in my mother's words / Dorothea Gutzeit.

"Irene Riznek ... recorded ... and prepared this autobiography"--Back cover. Issued in print and electronic formats.

ISBN 978-1-927032-49-7 (v. 1 : paperback).-- ISBN 978-1-927032-50-3 (v. 1 : pdf)

1. Gutzeit, Dorothea, 1921-2005. 2. Gutzeit, Dorothea, 1921-2005-- Family. 3. World War, 1939-1945--Germany. 4. Germany--History-- 1933-1945. 5. Germany--History--1945-1955. 6. Germans--Canada-- Biography. I. Riznek, Irene, transcriber, editor II. Title. III. Title: Be true and serve.

FC106 G3 G87 2016 971'.004310092 C2016-902957-3

C2016-902958-1

Design and editing Peter Geldart Danielle Aubrey Petra Books petrabooks.ca

978-1-927032-50-3 digital

978-1-927032-49-7 print

Dorothea Gutzeit
1921 - 2005

FOREWORD

by Irene Riznek (Koenigsberger)

My mother Dorothea, or Thea for short, was born in Berlin, Germany on March 10, 1921 in the Gutzeit family. She married Stimming and later Koenigsberger.

After my father's death in 1990, she courageously lived alone in a village farm house for many years. This farm house was many kilometres distance from her family. Although she kept in close contact with all by telephone, she was left with many long hours alone. I was aware of my mother's skill at the typewriter and I had even read an essay that she wrote for a writing course that she had once taken.

Often, when I took my children to visit their grandparents, the children would question my mother and father, as children some- times do. Their curiosity about their family's past often led to endless questions, and the stories that followed fascinated the listeners.

With my father's voice now silenced, I suggested that my mother pass some of her time with typing her memories. A strong-willed individual, my mother was not easy to influence. However after a little coaxing she revealed that she had kept some of the notes that she had written in response to my children's many questions years before. Overwhelmed and hesitant at putting one's thoughts and memories in writing, she asked "How do I begin?". To which I respond- ed, "Just type a page as the mood and memory hits you and I will help put it together at a later date." It was not until she suffered a stroke and I helped her clear the apartment to which she had moved when the farm house became too much, that my father's old war documents and the folder with those notes and some pages of memories came into my hands. We worked together for another two years. Although the typing is mine, the words are hers.

To assist in the writing of anyone's memoirs is a unique privilege, but to re-live your mother's experiences is a rare opportunity for personal introspection. Everyone has many sides and people are shaped by heredity and environment. All of us live in our personal moment, but we are also a part of a moment in history. While gather- ing and assimilating this narrative, I saw the impact of history and circumstance, and the definitive times in which my mother lived. The Second World War, for instance, affected and shaped an entire generation as well as each life uniquely.

As these pages began to reveal the full spectrum of the emotions of those times, I began to realize the tragedy and comedy of the world we live in. My mother often found herself in circumstances that were exhausting, and with energy drained, she was at times as emotional as any of us are. But true to the deep personal convictions of her youth and the influences of her favourite educator, Rector Schultz, her essence was to "BE TRUE AND SERVE", as clearly indicated by her efforts to provide better opportunities for her children and support of her husband.

All projects have a way of becoming more than they start out to be. What began as my mother's response to her grandchild's innocent questions about a grandmother's childhood home mushroomed into a story of grand proportions. Each of us has a story to tell. This is my mother's story.

TABLE OF CONTENTS

INTRODUCTION

by Dorothea

When my grandchildren were in their primary school years I would visit with them during their summer holidays. While walking hand-in-hand with my granddaughter, she would often ask questions about my childhood home. How big was the garden?... What did the house look like? ... and so on.

I started writing notes on my past in January 1986 when my granddaughter, a teen by then, became interested in my personal history and her ancestors. Later her brother became curious and questioned my husband about the war years. Time dwindled away and it wasn't until after my husband was gone, when time became too long and lonely for me, that my daughter suggested that I use my talents to record these precious memories so that they could be passed on to my descendants.

PRELUDE

My childhood nickname, Thea, stuck, and as I remember my childhood, I remember my tall and lean grandfather towering over his woodworking tools, forever busy with the large wood plane. Anorte, my grandmother, was short and round with a friendly face, endlessly patient with my sister Lisa and me during the summers on that farm in east Prussia.

As a child I would visit this farm and often imagine my mother and her childhood. How wonderful it must have been to grow up on this beautiful homestead set near the small quaint village. But my mother, at the age of 12, had an accident that shaped her future.

Often running barefoot, she stepped on some wood shavings left by my grandfather's work resulting in an injury that left her foot so badly cut that blood poisoning set in. There was fear that the leg might have to be amputated. Desperate and frightened, she made a pledge, vowing that if the leg healed without amputation, she would become a nurse.

The leg healed and when she turned 18 she kept her promise and enrolled at the Hamburg School of Nursing. Upon graduating, with the First World War imminent, she volunteered for service on the front lines. Stationed there, right at the front where the fighting was paramount, she was nurse to the many severely wounded Austrian, Hungarian and German soldiers. During my childhood I remember my mother often talking about the Russian front, about the terrible anxiety and fear when the fighting came too close, about the pain and anguish of the wounded and the horrible sights of the isolation ward for typhoid patients. She was so influenced by what she experienced and saw during her nursing career that she was adamant in dissuading any of her children from going into the nursing profession. However, one of her charges, Frieda, a stepdaughter, also followed the calling and went into nurse training as soon as she came of age and no longer required parental approval.

Germany was in turmoil and bankrupt. There was strife and struggle everywhere. In 1918, when my parents met the World War was barely over and had left a devastated Germany in ruins. But life is precious and the continuing search for happiness begins humbly with each new coupling. My mother and father served in that First World War and it was the circumstance and events of that time that led to my birth.

My mother, Auguste (Hertha) Wegner was born in 1892 and grew up in Lucknojen, (now called Neuenrode) in the county of Labiau, East Prussia, by the Baltic Sea. Her childhood was shaped by life on my grandfather's farm. But my grandfather was more than a farmer. He was a *Stellmacher*, a wheelwright. He made wood implements, rakes, wagon-wheels, axles, and even complete wagons. The work in his woodshop and the work on the small farm, which was utilized to its full capacity, kept my grandparents very busy. They grew their own vegetables, wheat, barley and oats. They had a horse to work the plow and cultivator. There were also a few cows, pigs, chickens and geese. It was a busy and thriving farm, although small. A long time before when my grandmother was young, it had been a huge farm of nearly 400 acres, but bit by bit my great-grandfather, who enjoyed the company of a bottle, drank it away until not much was left. My grandmother inherited the remnants of that farm, and this small six- acre plot of land was what I came to know as my grandparents' homestead.

My mother, a professional nurse for over ten years, had a career to be proud of — a true accomplishment and testament to her strength of character. She received many medals for her diligent military nursing during World War I and later received special honors for her work as a private nurse to Joachim, of the Austrian Royal House of Hapsburg. (Prince) Joachim, stationed at the Russian front, required extensive nursing care after what appeared to be an attempted suicide. A valiant prince who had had enough. World War I took its toll.

I remember admiring the medals as a child. I remember six of them proudly displayed in a little box. But those terrible times and the horrors of nursing at the WWI front lines were the building blocks that shaped my mother's attitude, and the courage that sustained her throughout her life and the struggles yet to come, when she was to survive another World War. At the time there was another nurse working in that military unit with my mother who had the same first name, Augusta. So my mother chose to be called Hertha and this name stuck for the rest of her life. It made things simpler as my father's name was August.

During my mother's first year of service she met Ernst Guenther, a field Chaplain and they fell in love. But this love affair turned tragic when Ernst contracted typhoid and despite my mother's attentive nursing, he died. It was his dying wish that my mother marry his best friend, August Gutzeit. August had two small daughters from a previous marriage and needed a wife and a mother for them. My mother eventually married August in 1920 but never forgot her first love. A picture of Ernst Guenther in his grey field uniform was always on display in our living room. If my father was hurt by this, he never allowed it to show but I'm sure there was a subtle sadness that my father suppressed. But then, after all, Ernst had been his best friend.

My father, August Gutzeit, was born in 1882 at Eystrup, County Hoya near the town of Goldap, which at that time was part of Poland. Orphaned at the age of four, he and his two brothers were raised, each in a different home, by friends of his parents.

His foster father was a highly qualified shoemaker who produced custom-made riding boots for cavalry officers. I remember my mother saying that she met this foster father only once, but that meeting left her with a lasting impression of a very distinguished gentleman.

Although my father picked up the art of shoemaking, he did not continue with that trade. However, once in later years he made my mother a beautiful pair of handmade shoes that I remember well.

During my childhood my father ensured that the whole family's shoes were polished to a glassy shine every Saturday and we never had to worry about worn shoes while we were growing up, for they were always immediately repaired. I still have my father's cobbler's knife in its well-worn leather sheath and my mind reflects on earlier times as I gaze at it.

Instead of shoemaking, my father made his career as a soldier and also served in the First World War. He was a cavalry officer with the 12th Ulanen Regiment of Insterburg. (12th Lancers Regiment of Insterburg.) There were three Mounted Regiments that were part of the German Army during WWI: The Husaren, The Dragoner and the Ulanen (Lancer Regiment.) All of these were very prestigious and famous regiments. So it was with great sadness that he accepted his retirement from the Lancers due to a leg injury he received when crushed by a horse. He was no longer able to ride, and in all my memories of him he always walked with his cane.

Regrettably, the documents and medals my father had received during his military career were taken, along with my mother's medals, by the Russian looters at the end of the Second World War. All that remains of his career is a water color painting depicting my father and fellow cavalry officers. This picture was painted by one of my father's friends, Hans Schramm, in 1934, and now proudly hangs in my son's home.

common oak, English oak, Moru Thomé, O.W., Flora von Deutschland Österreich und der Schweiz, Tafeln, vol. 2: t. 161 (1885) drawing: W. Müller
plantillustrations.org/illustration.php?id_illustration=149346

PART 1

GERMANY

1920 - 1959

The Berlin Cathedral (Oberpfarrund Domkirche von Berlin).
Completed in 1909, however much was destroyed by allied bombing in 1944. Located in East Berlin after the War, the temporary roof was replaced when reconstruction began in 1975.

ONE

1920 - 1932

Childhood and grand parents' farm

In 1920 my mother, Hertha, and my father, August, were married and moved to Berlin. They took an apartment at #13 Pettenkofer Strasse in the district of Friedrich's Hain. Ages before this district, the Hain, had been a hunting reserve for royal princes, but now it was a built up area right in the city centre of downtown Berlin. That move, to the urban congestion, must have been a shock for my mother who was raised on my grandparents' farm set in the middle of a beautiful conservation area within an old forest. The small fourth- floor walk-up apartment, with no trees, bushes or flowers anywhere in sight, was to become the newlywed's home.

When they married and moved to Berlin, they were an instant family, as the two girls from my father's first marriage were with them. Hertha was 12 years old and Frieda 10. Then, on March 10, 1921, I was born with the assistance of a midwife in that small apartment. My next three sisters were born in a hospital, so I imagine that the apartment delivery must have been a traumatic experience for my mother. The apartment was crowded, and as in all close living arrangements privacy can often be found by plunging oneself into a book. I was told that my older half-sister, Hertha, often looked after me with her book in one hand and rocking me in my baby carriage with the other. Once, being totally absorbed in her book, she never noticed that I had squirmed my way out and fallen to the floor. I was told that she continued rocking the baby carriage back and forth and I, being a quiet baby, I had fallen back to sleep there on the floor, with the carriage tire nudging my back. It was a silly incident but one that re-enforced my parent's desire to have a better place to bring up their children.

My parents were determined from the very beginning of their marriage to make their stay in that tiny apartment as short as possible, and set out a plan. Using every bit of savings that they had managed to keep from their army salary and nurse's pay, they bought a plot of land called a *morgen*. Aptly named a *morgen* because it is an area that could be ploughed by a horse in one morning, or *morgen*; this plot of land was on the outskirts of Berlin, in the district of Zehlendorf, well away from the congestion, apartments and traffic. Finding, and affording, this piece of land was a Godsend. It was in a fashionable district south-west of the city of Berlin and here one could feel the country air but still be able to access the city. But it was just a plot of land and needed a house. Now began months of daily commutes when my parents, with kids in tow, set out slowly but surely to build a small dwelling on that bit of land. The house began to take shape as three rooms and a kitchen were erected with an outhouse at the back. Although some areas of Berlin had sewer and hydro, these services did not come that far from the city proper. Hydro came in 1937 when I was in my mid teens. I remember it well, as it was my Saturday job to clean the petroleum lamps, polishing the reflectors and shining the delicate glass cylinders. The sewer was not connected until the early 1960's long after I was no longer residing there. We hated the out-house. It was dark and cold and you had to walk outside and around to the back of the house, where it was attached to the house but faced out into the back yard.

What was really amazing, however, was that my parents managed to build a house at all! Germany was in a desperate state. The monetary situation created inflation so great that one needed a wheel-barrow full of money to take to a store to buy a few staples. Everyone had to be creative, as well as work hard. My father was luckier than most of the unemployed during those terrible days. Because he had been a career soldier, he became eligible for a municipal job, and upon his release from the cavalry, due to his leg injury, he was given a job with the *S Bahn* or *Stadtbahn* (elevated city train).

To help one understand the current situation of those times it should be noted that Germany was bankrupt after the First World War. Inflation was ridiculously high and no matter how much money one had, nothing could be purchased. The money was worthless. The Treaty of Versailles, the armistice signed after the First World War was lost by the Germans, ensured that Germany would be responsible for payments to the victors, and those payments would have gone on forever! That Treaty also stated that there was be no trade with Germany. Germany was cut off. Inflation was uncontrollable, leaving the Reichsbank note valueless. Basically Germany had no economy, no future;

and with anarchy, chaos and depression all around, Germany was desperate.

One of Hitler's earliest official acts was to tear up the Treaty of Versailles and simply stop payments. He basically stated that the repatriation payments would be made with all the old currency, which was valueless anyway. And for German use, within Germany, he issued a new Deutsche Mark at a new value. He declared that Germany would become self sufficient! But the people needed food. There was an urgent need for fertilizer to grow faster and bigger crops and this piece of creative engineering had a strange side. It is interesting to note that the Haber process, developed by Fritz Haber, produced ammonia industrially within Germany. Ammonia was vital for agriculture as fertilizer but also had another use; it was used for the creation of explosives and munitions. Incidentally, F. Haber was the only person ever to be convicted as a war criminal and receive the Nobel Prize (1918) for the invention of the same process.

Hitler, with his concept of economics and his vision of a self- sufficient Germany, was able to create work and stimulate inventions thus providing jobs and food for the masses of unemployed Germans. Large-scale building and infrastructure work was begun. Museums, roads, bridges, monuments, government buildings and munitions factories were being built. Germany, under Hitler's regime, was able to pull itself out of a miserable depression towards a population with a near-zero unemployment rate.

Another part of the treaty, in effect after the First World War, was that Germany, although they had the *Wehrmacht* (defence force), they were not allowed to have an army exceeding 100,000 men. The depression had spawned anarchy, corruption and chaos. However, law and order was restored with the establishment of the new police force. Education and physical well-being was given a priority and sports became a keen interest for the young.

But all this came later and helped to shape my childhood.

First, my newly-married parents planned and worked to provide a house and home with a garden to help feed their new family. Marriage and family, during the hardships of this depression, was a challenge within itself. The garden was to supplement the food that was so expensive to buy. My parents were enterprising and hard- working and so they managed. While my mother organized and worked the garden, my father built the house, almost single- handedly, with the exception of the aid of my mother's brother Otto. He worked in the building industry and would come by to help whenever he could, giving advice and sometimes clues as to where builders were selling scrap.

As our family grew, another room was added and then later a laundry room at the back of the house, and later still the attic was expanded to provide a second floor. Demolition sites were scoured to provide some of the necessary building materials. The lovely double door with the glass window that was later added to divide the main floor living quarters from the front hall was purchased second-hand from one of these sites. That door still graces the entrance to the main floor rooms to this very day.

I was only three years old and my sister Elisabeth (Lisa) not quite twelve months of age, when we finally moved to our place in Zehlendorf. Small as I was, I remember that the door to the kitchen had a hole where the door knob was supposed to be. It was many years before the rope that was tied through the hole and served as a door pull was replaced with a proper door handle. But much of what I remember of that move is what was told to me rather than actual memories.

My mother sold her ear-rings and silver flatware that she had received as a wedding gift from her mother, Anorte Wegner. She kept only six teaspoons with the monogram A/W and these are still with the family today. The money from the sale was used to buy fruit trees, berry bushes, vegetable and flower plants. From my earliest memories, I can remember that the large garden seemed like a huge park-like oasis for me. My mother did all the work herself except for handling the heavy spade that was used to hand-till what today would be a very large garden. My father, who grew up in the town of Goldap in East-Prussia, had no experience with gardening but he handled the spade and soon learned how to prune the many fruit trees. His preferred hobbies, however, were raising the rabbits and pigeons, and he belonged to breeder clubs for both. Beside the rabbits and pigeons we had hens for the eggs, one or two ducks, some turkeys and a goat for milk. At one time we also had a large watch-dog but this didn't work out too well. He was a beautiful German Sheppard who preferred to lie under the dining room table, coming to life whenever we had visitors and then only to beg to be stroked and petted. The rest of the time he would affectionately rub his nose and shoulders against our legs, as we sat at the dining room table, until he felt a hand stroking him. Not much of a watch dog! So my mother, a practical and thrifty woman, who decided that every- thing should have its purpose, stated that he was to be given away.

It is easy to imagine that this plot of land with all its trees, bushes, flowers and many animals was a paradise for my sister and me. As my mother was great at preserving everything, we had fresh fruits and vegetables all year around. For us children the fresh eggs, delicious rabbit stew, and fried chicken were certainly wonderful, but the best part was that we could play with the animals and we soon learned to look after them. Our favorite "play" animal was a kid, the only off-spring our goat had. Lisa and I loved that baby goat and one cold, wet evening our hearts felt for this poor thing outside in the rain. While Lisa and I were supposed to be sleeping, we devised a secret way to get the baby goat inside. Ever-so quietly we put the ironing board out through our ground floor bedroom window and coaxed the little goat to climb up and inside. After a quick shake it promptly made itself comfortable on our bed and slept with us for the night. In the morning, very early before dawn, we took care to have it back outside. We were happy that we had kept the little goat dry and warm during the night and that we were able to get it back out so early before anyone would notice; satisfied and secure in our little secret, we thought no one would be aware that the goat had been in our bed. But my mother could smell it as soon as she came to wake us, and despite her disapproval as she took in the full spectrum of the muddy floor, the bed sheets, and wet goat smell, she had to suppress a laugh. Although we escaped punishment we were not allowed to play with the goat again.

The only fly in this veritable honey pot was my baby cousin, Max- Walter. His mother Anna, my mother's sister, died at his birth. My mother went to East-Prussia and brought Max-Walter back to be with our family. That alone did not bother me, but that he occupied my beloved doll bed was the reason for many tears and stormy protests on my part. Poor Max-Walter was only a few months old when he died of meningitis and so I got my doll bed back. But by then I was so guilt-ridden, believing that my resentment caused his death, that I never put my doll in that little bed again.

Those golden, early child-hood years appeared to go on forever. But soon my whole life changed as I started school, and I loved it from day one. At that time, in the 1920s and 1930s, school started at eight o'clock in the morning and went till noon, with the higher classes staying until one o'clock. Getting to and from school meant a thirty-minute walk each way as there were no school buses. The school, *Sued Schule* (south school), to which I and my sisters, and later my own three children went, was considered the best school near and far. The teachers and especially the Rector (principal) were tremendously dedicated and outstanding educators. I credit them with instilling in me the desire and love of learning, to read and to take an everlasting interest in world history, geography and philosophy. Rector Schultz, an extraordinary educator, hand-picked his staff, giving us the best selection of teachers available. Parents from all over Berlin were pressing to have their children enrolled in *Sued Schule*. The students came by *S Bahn* and city bus. Some of the teachers were so progressive that I didn't realize how much until I was well into my adulthood.

Mr. Streese, our Geography teacher taught us about earth physics, the inevitable shift of the earth's axis and the tectonic plates. Our physical education teacher, Mr. Dabisch, had a very peculiar method of exercising that he taught to us. I didn't realize until much later in life that it was Yoga! Our History teacher, Mr. Mueller, kept us spellbound by making us relive history in our imaginations. Often, at 8:00 in the morning, the first class of the day began when it was still dark outside. Leaving the lights off, Mr. Mueller fascinated us with history stories in the dark. Many of these teachers became close friends with our family thereby extending the education process into our home and around the dinner table. We benefited, and they benefited with the many gifts of fruit and vegetables that my mother gave them from our garden.

As I write this, it is September 2000, and my great-grand- daughter is excitedly telling me about the new school year and her anticipation of starting the first grade. That brings back memories of a German custom regarding the very first day of school. At the introductory day's end, after the children have spent the first few hours at school, they are let out to greet their anxiously awaiting parents or care-givers. The children are met with smiles and a gift. Each child is presented with a huge, brightly colored papier-mâché cone decorated with shiny paper and stickers. Each cone is as varied as the children to whom they are given. Upon opening the ribbon that ties it all together, the children find the cone filled with all sorts of goodies. There are the usual candies and chocolates but also some practical gifts such as a hairbrush, crayons, pencils, and maybe even a small toy. Some of the papier-mâché cones are as large as the children are tall. The children eagerly anticipate this gift and its aim was to help them get over the strangeness and stress of that first school day.

As I look back and compare the school systems of today with the school system of my youth, I must admit there is another thing I preferred about school in my time. The students did not have to wander from room to room for each different subject. We stayed in our class-room and the different teachers came to us. The exceptions were music, physical education and chemistry classes. In retrospect another thing I value and appreciate is that our *Klassenlehrer* (home or form teacher) stayed with us from grade one to the end of the school years, right through to graduation. The teacher knew each student intimately, knowing his or her strengths or weaknesses, and it was generally held that the teacher could help to develop the potential of the student through the years.

During my youth, great emphasis was placed on physical education. There were at least two periods every week during which we used the very well-equipped exercise room, that we called a *Turnhalle*, which was equipped with everything that a gymnast could possibly dream of, and the equipment was well used. In addition there were extra-curricular voluntary sports where one could participate in game

sports such as *Fussball*, or Handball all with the intent of providing a well-rounded physical education to supplement the high standards of classroom work. During these years I became so interested in sports, especially track and field, that I joined a sports club. Two afternoons a week you would find me on the sports field, practicing discus and javelin throwing, doing the 100-meter dash or 400-meter hurdles, broad and high jumps. On top of that, my father enrolled me with a rowing team stationed on the beautiful Wannsee, one of the many lakes around the city of Berlin. With all that training afternoons and most Saturdays I became very busy. In fact I was so busy with sports, that it absolved me from many household chores which suited me just fine. My sister Lisa, who was not athletically inclined, got stuck with them most of the time. Of course I did have to help in the house and garden too, but since I preferred outside work, I managed to be of more help during harvest time. Harvesting was a time - consuming job that kept me working for long hours, picking the various berries, cherries, apples and so on, as we had at least 40 currant bushes, an equal number of gooseberry bushes, as well as the many cherry, apple, plum and pear trees. The harvested fruit was canned for our own use, but the rest, and it was a great deal more than just a bit, was sold by my parents to wholesalers thereby supplementing the family income. Under my mother's supervision and cultivation, the garden was so productive that my father was also kept busy, as he made wine from the different fruits and became so proficient in wine making that his product was much in demand by my parent's friends!

As my mind turns back to the track and field events, I remember two annual events over and above the regular competitive meets with other clubs. They were *abturnen* and *anturnen*. *Anturnen* happened in early Spring, on the first day the sports field was opened and *abturnen* on the last day of use, towards fall. Each event was a friendly competition between the members of the sports clubs. Our club was named *Z-88*, meaning *Zehlendorf* 1888, the year the club was formed. This gives an idea of the importance that physical education had in Germany, an importance instilled in all children from an early age on.

I became quite good at track and field. I was one of the girls chosen to represent our club at a province-wide competition. I captured second place and was proud of myself and still have the prestigious bronze Oak Leaf Medal after all these years. The relay team, of which I was a member, also won several competitions with other clubs. All this diverse athletic training opened the doors in later years when I became the sports manager in a large firm, where I found work after leaving school, and continued to work, before and after the war, but more about this later.

My parents favored an all-round education and as soon as the time was right my father bought season tickets to the opera and theater for me. Both events were sponsored and supervised through the school. When my sister Lisa was old enough, she was given season tickets as well. However, regrettably for my later siblings, life and education would not be the same. The first opera I attended was Bizet's Carmen. This made a deep impression on me and this opera has remained my favorite throughout my life. The last time I saw Bizet's Carmen was in June 1994 in Berlin with my favorite tenor, Jose Carreras. I am still an opera fan and have several opera on video, among them Carmen, naturally, and Don Carlos, Stiffelio and Andrea Chernier. As I write this, I am now 79 years old, but my love for opera music is as fresh as ever. I have many CDs with opera music, mostly tenors singing these beautiful arias; I am always amazed at the beauty of the human voice.

Another aspect of my schooling that appealed to me was the large garden plot behind the school. Those students interested in garden- ing were allowed to cultivate a section of it. Despite the huge garden we had at home, I wanted a plot of my own. At home it was difficult for me to have my own plot. Firstly, every little spot was utilized for growing valuable food crops and secondly, my mother was too impatient and much too busy to spend time showing me the ropes. So I planted my little plot at the school but not with crops, just with flowers. I planted so many marigolds, asters, snapdragons and other blooming plants that my plot looked like a miniature jungle. In later years, wherever I lived, I always had a garden with many flowers. Now in my old age, I have a thirteen-meter-long balcony which during the summer months is an oasis of green and color. My daughter Irene is helpful with planting and carrying the many varieties of the most delicate plants, earth and various garden pots up to the 13th floor balcony, but I assure her that every effort is worth the many hours of enjoyment as I read or write near the fragrant blooms. Although my old school in Berlin-Zehlendorf is still there, the garden plot does not exist anymore. Now it is built up with houses, as is the sports field, and it saddens me that the students no longer have easy access to those green open spaces.

It is easy to see that school played a great part in my young life and I loved every minute of it. I was lucky that I had teachers who were dedicated educators instilling in me a love of learning and quest for knowledge that is with me even to this day. Now, when I am not as mobile as I used to be, books are my favored companions and I am happy that my children and grand children enjoy reading as well.

My wonderful childhood years are full of happy memories but not without incident. I was slow to anger but my temper, once provoked, made me quick to react especially if I felt I had been wronged.

My mother, although she had enough hard work in her own garden, somehow found time to supplement her own garden produce income by helping another gardener. This man's son became my friend and even though we were both only six years of age we played at yard work together and often he became my companion as we walked to school. Once en route to school we passed a building site with many bricks strewn about. In youthful glee he picked one up and threw it in my direction, narrowly missing me. Immediately I picked up that same brick and threw it back. Unfortunately it hit him smack in the middle of his forehead leaving a huge bleeding gash. As he ran home to his mother, his father swiftly cycled to my home and reported my temper. I arrived home to an extremely angered atmosphere and was severely reprimanded as I could have seriously injured this young boy's head. While my mother shouted and spanked me, I began to analyze and think things through. I was still not quite sure where I had gone wrong, because after all, he threw first!

He and I still played together and I ran into trouble again. We were all turning earth with a pitch fork. Though my friend and I were merely playing, we felt that we were helping. When his father called him to come home my friend lifted his arm to push the pitchfork into the ground hoping to leave it standing upright. He missed and pushed it directly into his own foot. As I was standing nearby his father once again accused me of causing this accident. The father shouted that every time I was around something happens. I was left feeling frustrated and insecure.

Trouble seemed to follow me. At the age of eight I had the thickest, longest and most beautiful blond braids. I think because I was quiet, studious and always the head of the class, I was not too well liked. Once, while concentrating on my studies at my school desk, the fellow who sat behind me dipped my beautiful braid into the open ink well that was on everyone's desk. With swift reaction I grabbed my open ink well and threw it at his face. For this horrific action I was told to stand in the classroom corner. Standing there, humiliated for the entire period I couldn't help but wonder why *he* was not punished. Anger and outrage stewed inside my head.

Although I was studious and enjoyed my teachers, it was my summers spent on my grandmother's farm that bring back the warmest emotions.

My father, who worked for the S *Bahn* (elevated city railway), was entitled to two free railway passes every year for each member of his family. We used these train passes when we accompanied my mother on her visit to her parents' farm in East-Prussia. My mother would take my sister Lisa and myself, stay for a few days, and then go back home leaving us behind with our grandparents. She could never stay for any length of time because of the demands of the house and the huge garden, and also by this time my younger sister, Christa, was born. And so, as soon as I was old enough, I was entrusted to look after Lisa, two years younger than I, as we were sent off, by ourselves, by train, to spend the long summer holidays in East- Prussia. This visit with my grandparents was always one of the highlights of the year and full of exciting adventures that began with the long train ride.

As I think back today to all the Slavic towns and villages we passed through, I recall all their old Slavic names. Hitler changed these names as he considered anything Slavic inferior. Then Russia, Poland and the other states changed the names again at the conclusion of World War II, adding much to my confusion when comparing old maps.

East-Prussia was an area between Poland, Russia and the Baltic Sea. The Polish Corridor was established after the 1st World War to give Poland, which was land-locked, access to the Baltic Sea. With this geographical adjustment Danzig, now Gdansk, became a German enclave. To go to my grandparents the train on which we travelled went straight through this corridor. During the entire time that the train spent in the Polish Corridor all the blinds were drawn. The local politics of that time decreed that anyone who was not of Polish origin should not be allowed to look out.

We always travelled from Berlin to Koenigsberg, now Kaliningrad, where we had to change to a slower local train and travel on to our next stop at Szargillen. Our grandfather always met us with a horse and wagon, and after that it was still another hour's wagon ride through the most beautiful and enchanting forest till we came to my grandparents' farm.

On one occasion the local train was full of farmers all speaking in varied and accented dialects. We were listening with such absorbed fascination that we forgot to get off at Szargillen and proceeded on to Laukischken. Here the station master took us into the ticket office where we spent the night trying to sleep with our heads tucked on our arms as we sat stretched across the wooden table. But it was not just this discomfort that kept us from sleeping. The station master happened to be a woman and she was entertaining her boyfriend! The two were smooching and necking all night while we pretended to sleep. Then, in the wee morning hours, near four am, it was arranged for us to accompany a farmer whose job it was to pick up the various milk cans that dairy farmers had left by the roadside. Lucknojen, right by my grandparents' farm, was on his route.

There was so much at my grandparents' farm that kept us entertained. There were all the animals, the cows and pigs, the horse Sam, the geese and chickens. And there were the children from the village. For them, my sister and I were a novelty because we came from "the big city". We dressed differently, spoke differently, and always had books with us to read to them. Often we would all sit in the fields by the little pond, with the geese nearby cropping the luscious grass, while I read aloud.

Sam was a working horse which when hitched to a wagon or other farm implement, was doing the work a tractor would do now-a- days. He was also a patient and friendly horse, and would allow us children, one at a time, to sit on his back while he was working. In exchange for these rides my sister and I brushed and cleaned him so that his hide gleamed and we always had a carrot or another tidbit treat for him. Our childhood summers were carefree and happy as we absorbed country life.

My grandmother, who was always busy, entertained us as we observed and learned. We watched with fascination the process of bread baking with sourdough. The dough was mixed in a large wooden trough the evening before and left to stand over night. The next morning the huge brick oven in the kitchen was heated with birch wood that gave the large round bread a taste that was divine! When the wood had burned to ashes and the walls in the oven were too hot to touch, the ashes and the rest of the wood were swept out with a corn broom. The loaves were molded and shaped into neat round mounds and then shoved into the swept-out oven with wooden paddles and baked. When the bread was done and with the oven still hot enough, a more delicate cake was baked in it. As soon as the bread was cool enough to touch we were each handed a huge slice spread with slabs of home-churned butter. I will never forget the taste of this bread as we gorged ourselves with this delicious treat.

We were allowed to take turns churning the butter. First the cream was poured into a cylindrical wood container, narrow at the top and fitted with something like a giant potato masher. Then gripping it firmly with both hands, the masher was plunged rapidly up and down until the cream solidified. As the cream separated and turned to chunks, more and more physical strength was required and we could not do it for very long. Tiring quickly, we gave the chore back to my grandmother and continued watching until eventually she would scoop out the lumps of butter which were molded roughly into bricks, wrapped in a damp cheesecloth and placed on a board in the cooling room, or milk room, to store.

The butter we buy today cannot compare with the sweet taste of home-churned butter! When we once again left for home, we were always allowed to take some lumps of churned butter with us. But the lumps were not the real gift. The taste of the bread and butter and my memories of those carefree days on the farm, those were the precious gifts I took home with me.

Hours and hours were spent playing with those farm animals. We would take the geese to the pond in the middle of the village and watch over them. But one of our favorite pastimes, especially when it was very hot, was to take the old-fashioned metal bath tub to the garden. Then we gathered all the little piglets we could and proceeded to wash them. The squealing and scrambling was accentuated with our hysterical laughter. But it is not that we were always kind; we were normal kids and also mischievous. Once we took a goose and tied her to the huge hay wagon wheel. Luckily grandmother saw and came to the goose's rescue before any damage was done, as my grandfather was about to drive off.

Clear memories of the attic above the little one-story stone farm- house come back to me. I can remember my grandmother sitting there on her loom where she would weave the most extraordinary things. There is an embroidered dresser scarf that I, in my later years, cut into three so that each of my children would have a piece of this hand-woven cloth. This cloth was a piece of a huge bedspread woven by my grandmother. I embroidered each of the three pieces to finish the rough edges and repair the ancient material.

In that attic was a large wooden bin where the wheat was stored. And by the huge chimney that came through the attic from the kitchen, bacon and ham hung to cure and smoke. There was always a delicious smell similar to a slow-roasting barbeque in that attic. Often I would sit there on a small three-legged stool that my grand- father had made for me, surrounded by that wonderful aroma and watch my grandmother weave, as I read her my favorite stories.

The animals needed hay for winter feeding and my grandfather rented some meadows on the Kurische Haff, a large bay on the Baltic Sea. The grass on this peninsula was especially sweet and good for making hay. It took over an hour-and-a-half ride with horse and wagon through dense forest to get to the shore of the Baltic Sea. Then, once at the bay, we parked our wagon and tethered the horse while we continued on a large fishing boat over the Haff to reach the peninsula where the field was. Around hay-making time we were allowed to come with my grandfather and my uncle and aunt to "help". The cut grass had to be turned several times to allow it to dry well and that, of course, was where we "helped". Hay-making time was always an anxious time for my grandfather because if it should rain during those few days, when the hay lay cut, it was ruined. Bringing the dry hay home was another chore. First it was loaded onto the boat and then transferred to the wagon and all this was done without the aid of any of our fancy modern equipment that farmers have to help them today. It took strong arms to shovel pitch fork after pitch fork onto the boat and then again, when transferred onto the wagon. And then, to our great joy, we were allowed to ride all the way home sitting on our lofty perch on top of this mountain of hay.

We took other trips during the year in addition to our summer holidays at that farm in East Prussia. At Easter or during the Fall holidays, my sister Lisa and I were sent to a camp or a youth home which was operated and supervised by the Lutheran Church. As these camps were in different parts of Germany, I was able to visit the Black Forest, Thuringia, Saxony, Bremen, and the Baltic Sea. I was often homesick during those early excursions and I was glad once my sister was old enough to come with me.

I am mentioning my sister Lisa a lot as she was only two years younger than I and we spent much time together. My little sister, Christa, was seven years, seven months younger.

When Christa was just a baby she had a terrible accident. She was sitting among the cushions in her carriage near the table and somehow managed to pull a freshly brewed pot of hot coffee over her legs. A large ugly burn on her leg behind the knee left her in agony. Christa was hospitalized for a long time, and until she was fully grown, had to have skin grafts periodically as that huge scar did not grow with her. The initial healing period was very long and we had to be especially careful with her.

The year this accident happened was also the year my young cousin Gerd came into our life. My mother's younger sister, eighteen years old at the time, had come to Berlin to find work. She became pregnant and in those days the pressure and stigma of being an unmarried single mother was tremendous. She shot herself leaving her new-born son behind. My mother took the baby and cared for Gerd, raising him with us. He was closest in age to Christa and they became fast friends. And so the house became ever-more a home to the many inhabitants. It was alive with people and children of all ages; Hertha, Frieda, myself, Lisa, Christa, Gerd, and with the many chores, different personalities, and the comings and goings, there was always excitement.

During the time of Christa's accident and later during her many skin-graft convalescence, my eldest half-sister, Hertha, who worked as a sales lady for a large department store and later lived in a flat of her own, would often came to visit us. During those visits she took special care of Christa and was very patient with her. Yet, always remembering the rest of us children, she would bring sweets and spend time telling us tales of her work and life on her own. We were enchanted, but really enjoyed the little chocolate figures filled with sweet cream the best.

As soon as I was able to read I was never without a book. Not only did it provide privacy and escape into new worlds, but it could also be very helpful in keeping Christa quiet. I loved reading and Christa was a good listener. She would be very still, quietly watching my face as my voice would go up and down as I made the characters in the book come to life. Christa could thus be occupied quietly, avoiding further leg injury and I was useful doing what I loved — reading.

In those early childhood years my mother could make an ordinary Sunday into a celebratory feast and calendar holidays became special celebrations. I'm sure there was a lot of extra effort and work involved for my mother, who was busy enough, but she always made these occasions extra special with traditions and ceremony. I know of no other culture, except the Jewish culture, that keeps traditions and holidays with the passion that knits a family together with a united, loving and spiritual focus. For my mother, faith and family were most important and Sunday was a special day.

December was a special month, beginning with December 6th, St. Nicholas Day. As children we knew the story well. The story goes that St. Nicholas went to visit poor children with gifts of food and toys. He carried the gifts in a sack over his shoulder. On the evening of December 5th, the day before St Nicholas Day, my mother insisted that each of us children polish one of our shoes, until you could mirror your face in it. Into this shoe we put a wish list, which we had prepared very carefully, mentioning our special Christmas wishes without appearing too greedy. We placed the polished shoe, with the note, carefully at the foot of our bed. The next morning, the wish list was gone and the shoe was filled with lots of goodies: an apple or an orange, Christmas cookies, sweets and sometimes a tiny gift. We always tried to stay awake during this special night hoping to see St Nicholas, but we never did.

The four Sundays before Christmas, called the Advent Sundays, were also special. As we were devout Christians, we always went to church on Sundays, but on these Advent Sundays there was a special church service with festive music, and often the children of the congregation would participate with a short recital or children's choir. A pine-branch wreath hung from great ribbons over the altar. On it were four large candles. On the First Advent Sunday one candle would be lit and we would watch it flicker as the pastor delivered his sermon. At the end of the service it would be nothing but a small stump, and would be replaced for the Second Advent Sunday when two candles would be lit for the sermon. And so it would be until the Fourth Advent Sunday, the Sunday just before Christmas, when the wreath at Church would cast a beautiful glow with all four candles lit. At home we had our own Advent wreath, laboriously made ahead of time with branches, ribbons and decorations. Once home from church we would light a candle and enjoy our meal in our living room, afterwards playing and entertaining ourselves with music and games until the last glow of the candle was gone. The next Advent Sunday there would be two candles and so the living room took on a festive air that would last through December until the last Advent Sunday when all the candles would be lit in anticipation of Christmas Eve.

My mother took care to bake extra -special cookies and cakes for these four Advent Sundays. The children were allowed to help with the baking, licking the bowls and tasting the still-warm cookies. My mother was a terrific cook, but seemed particularly so during the Christmas season when there was a special aroma all through the house of apples, nuts, cookies and spicy baking smells.

When the day of Christmas Eve came, we were not allowed to go into the living room. My father would bring in the tree and my mother would decorate it and place the gifts. All this was done in secret during Christmas Eve. We children would sit in the kitchen, each with one gift to occupy us. For me it was always a book. There was much coming and going by my parents and sometimes there were noises that we could not identify. When we were young and asked what all the noise was about in the living room, we were told that it was the Christmas angels coming and going.

Finally once darkness had come, a little bell tinkled as my mother beckoned us to the open door of the living room. Every year in my youth is was the same. Every year we stood awestruck at the door and looked at the decorated tree, blazing with candles that threw shadows on the walls and ceiling of the darkened room. There, spread out on the dining table were our gifts. The gifts were not wrapped but instead they were beautifully displayed with colorful ribbons that flared out from the table centre-piece, sectioning off each child's special area laden with gifts. In the centre of each of our sections, each one of us had a brightly decorated paper plate called the *bunte teller* full of cookies, apples, nuts and other sweets. We always knew which was our gift section but there was no rushing towards the gifts. First we all sat down and listened to my father or mother read the Christmas story from the family Bible. Then each child recited a poem appropriate for the season and, only after the whole family sang Christmas carols together, were we allowed to go to our gifts. After many Ohs and Ahs, some disappointments and much joy, we had a light supper which was always prepared in advance. Then we dressed warmly and went to the Midnight church service. All this happened on Christmas Eve.

We attended another church service on Christmas morning, and often visitors came in the afternoon. Our family was seldom alone for the festive Christmas day dinner which was always a goose with all the trimmings. On the second Christmas day, which in America is called 'boxing day', we went visiting and took gifts to our relatives and friends. Baked goods were exchanged and every woman tried to outdo the other with fancy cakes and cookies.

That beautiful Christmas tree stayed up until New Year's and every night until New Year's Eve the candles on the Christmas tree were lit and we enjoyed playing with our gifts in the living room in that festive atmosphere. It might sound strange to you that we did not have electric lights, and always used lit candles, yet for as long as I lived in Germany, there was never an accident with them. I suppose we were accustomed to the extra attention open flames required. Many years later, when I lived in the upstairs rooms of that same house, long after my own children were born, and my mother and sisters lived downstairs, my mother ensured that these special Christmas celebrations continued, even when I too had become a mother. I'm sure even my youngest, Irene, who was almost seven years old when we left this house, can remember these festivities.

When New Year's Eve came we were ready for celebrations of a different flavor. It was another festive day but now full of anticipation for midnight. We played board games to 'kill' the time. We melted small lumps of lead and dumped them into ice cold water to see what shape they would take. With lots of imagination we would predict the future from them, as each of us in turn toyed with the idea of what the next year would bring. Then, a few minutes before midnight, we all went outside. Excitedly we watched as father lit the roman candles. We would watch and listen to the ringing church bells which filled the night all around. Some people had fireworks in their gardens and all-in-all I remember the emotionally moving moments when we greeted the New Year.

The main event on New Year's Day was the 'plundering' or dismantling of the Christmas tree. Even this became a celebration. The tree, which was decorated with the traditional glass balls, stars and figurines, was also hung with all sorts of sweets: chocolate pretzels, marzipan, and cookies. Once again we were filling our *bunte teller*, those fancy Christmas paper plates, with all the tree's goodies and now gorging ourselves on New Year sweets.

In the days when the economy was tight and technology not advanced enough to take away innocent pleasures, and much before there was any inkling of the impending war, my mother was terrific at creating beautiful memories of special events.

I remember Easter celebrations, that I and my siblings would look forward to. This feast fell in a season when the first flowers, tulips, daffodils, and crocus were already blooming, and Easter festivities seemed to add to the natural excitement of Spring. Long before we were awake, my mother would be baking special Easter bread. The warm smell of baking with the aroma of freshly-brewed coffee mingling with the smoke of my father's Sunday cigar would greet us as we awoke. Easter morning always started with an elaborate breakfast and then, right after breakfast, and for most of early Easter morning, we children were banned to the back yard. There we waited for the time to pass, swinging on our wooden rope swings hanging from the fruit trees. We were told not to mess up our Sunday clothes

… what torture. After a seemingly endless time we were finally called to the front of the house and the Easter-egg hunt was on. Each of us was allotted a certain area of the garden in which to search for the Easter eggs which had been skillfully hidden among the flowers and greenery. I have fond memories of Easter particularly because of this Easter-egg hunt, and the laughing and dashing about and shouting "I found one!", and then we were off to church.

Our family was by no means well off, but at these feasts, Christmas, Easter or birthdays, my mother created such an atmosphere that we felt rich. My parents were very careful with their money; my mother augmented my father's salary by working Spring and Summers at a nursery as well as selling produce from our garden. Although she was busy with chores in her garden, the house, and all the while looking after a home full of children, I never had the feeling that I was missing anything. We ate well, we always had books to read and our garden supplied a bountiful harvest to sell, even having some to share with friends and neighbors.

Education was very important in our family and our parents provided us with every opportunity to learn. There were always books lying around, begging to be read. At a very young age I was reading Kiekegard, Rabindranath Tagore, Goethe, Maria Rilke etc. Some of the books went over my head and made me want to know more.

So I read. Often I would sneak to some hiding place with a book and avoid household duties. My favorite hiding place was up an old, dense apple tree. You really had to look hard to find me there, and when I was reading I was lost to the world. Later, my own small children soon found that out. One day, while I was deep into a book, I heard one say to the other, "let's go, mum is reading, she won't know". That immediately brought my attention back to reality and I was more careful with my reading during my children's waking hours.

In 1933, I was twelve years old and nearing the end of my child- hood. It was an important year in my young life, but this year also marked the beginning of some changes in our family, and on a broad- er scale, major changes in Germany and by extension to the world.

On the 30th of January, 1933, President Von Hindenburg appoint- ed Adolf Hitler as chancellor of Germany. But for me it was the beginning of the two-year confirmation class. My family belonged to the Lutheran Church and church played an important part in our lives. Every Sunday after Sunday school, we stayed for the Church service where we were joined by our parents. Sunday was always a festive day. We were dressed in our "Sunday best" and had an elaborate Sunday midday meal which was often followed with a glass of wine. Father smoked his weekly cigar and in the afternoon we all had coffee and cake. Other than feeding the animals, there was no work to be done on Sunday. We read, played games and generally had a good time. Sometimes our father would take us to a museum or an open-air Sunday concert. My father wanted to share his passion for live music concerts, performing Renaissance, Classical and popular music with us whenever he could. Once on Pentecost, a three-day holiday in Germany, father and I got up very, very early to pedal our bicycles to a restaurant on the shores of the "Krumme Lanke", a lake in Zehlendorf. We wanted to be sure of a good spot as we ate our breakfast and listened to the morning concert of a brass band playing the popular music of that era.

I was the oldest of my immediate siblings and as such I was fortunate to accompany my father on his trips to visit his older daughter, Hertha who was by now grown up and married. Her husband Willy was a seaman and Chef on board the ocean liner "Bremen". He was proud to sail on the Bremen, which won the prestigious Blue Ribbon award three times, for being the fastest ship crossing the Atlantic from Bremerhaven to New York. I remember well the day my father and I had our photos taken on the deck of the Bremen. I felt as excited and as important as only a thirteen year old could.

Willy was to sail on the Bremen until it was sunk in Murmask North Russia, in the Arctic Circle in 1941. Germany was not yet at war with the Russians but there were rumors that the non-aggression pact with Germany and Russia might not work. I am not quite sure how or who ordered the crew off the Bremen and told them to go home. The ship was then set on fire and sunk. Willy somehow made his way back to Germany and later sailed as chief cook on the Greek ocean liner "Columbia". I mention this now, not just as a fond memory of an outing with my father, but also because Willy played an import- ant role later in my life that was pivotal in determining my future.

But I'm getting ahead of myself; I want to take you back to the year 1933 and my Confirmation. Our weekly Sunday school lessons prepared me somewhat for the confirmation classes. However, with my inquisitive mind going full gear, there were many things taught in confirmation class that I could not fully accept. Our pastor found that I was disturbing the other children with my many questions and decided to instruct me privately in our home. I soon looked forward to those hours as the pastor was fluent in Hebrew and Greek and could refer to earlier translations of the Bible in order to answer my queries. Learning a great deal from him, gave me a clearer under- standing of the Bible and the meaning of religion. He paved the way for my ongoing quest for the truth of Spirituality as opposed to religions. He informed my parents that the customary two years of instructions were not necessary for me and so I was confirmed at the age of thirteen.

TWO

1933 - 1938

Teen years; tensions growing

Germany in 1933, beginning with Hitler's chancellorship, was experiencing some sweeping changes. The electrifying effect that this year had was felt at home through school. Isolated and vivid memories creep forward. Here I will include a story that I had written during my adulthood for an essay that I had prepared for a writing course. "Be True and Serve" was the title I chose for this essay, as it best reflects the core of what became the force that sustains me, for it is often the teen years that mold and shape the adult.

I remember the day my mother was brushing my hair before school. I was twelve years old and my mother was arranging my thick hair into the beautiful long braids that made me feel neat and well-groomed. I gritted my teeth and held my breath until tears stung my eyes, but I would rather have burst than show a sign of pain. How could I afford to miss one word, one syllable of the most interesting, amazing conversation going on over my head — literally over my head — because I was sitting on the low three-legged wooden stool which my father used on Sunday mornings as he polished and repaired the family's shoes. My mother was combing and brushing my long hair trying to get every stray and tangled strand smoothly into a thick braid. My head went rhythmically back and forth with every vigorous stroke of the brush, and I found it almost impossible to focus my eyes on the figure of the elderly woman just outside the kitchen window. I wanted so much to see Granny Becker's face and her reaction to my mother's most unbelievable and fascinating burst of anger.

Granny Becker lived in two small rooms at the back of our house. In return for odd jobs in our home and the large garden, she enjoyed the privilege of a very low rent and the stimulating company of a vigorous young family. She had just finished listening to the crack- ling of her battery-operated radio and had counted on her fingers in wonderment the honors to be bestowed that very day upon our leader Adolf Hitler. Each announcement of special events to take place in different parts of Berlin, in celebration of his birthday, was framed in crisp-march music and folk songs. Granny Becker had only nine fingers, the tenth left behind on her father's farm in East Prussia when a heavy door swung shut. When the tenth event was mentioned she turned her radio off and came shuffling around the house to the open kitchen window from where came the same flow of march music and announcements from my mother's radio.

Granny Becker leaned over the low window sill and motioned to my mother until she had her attention. Mother turned the radio down a bit and asked; "What did you say, Granny Becker?"

"I just said, isn't it a bit too much fussing around about the chancellor? The way they carry on with him, one would think he is God in person. All that is left is to put him on a pedestal and fall down and worship him."

Mother stopped short and with a jerk she pulled the half finished braid taut, making me wince again. She straightened herself up to her fullest height and instead of agreeing with Granny Becker, as I had expected her to do, she exploded with these angry words that I was amazed to hear from her.

"Mrs. Becker, not granny this time, I want you to know that there is not enough that could possibly be done to show our gratitude to our Leader! God himself has sent him to help Germany out of the misery of depression, frustration and hunger. Have you already forgotten, Mrs. Becker, how we prayed during our Tuesday gospel hours for help? For some help, for us and for all the others who were hungry, lonesome and frightened? Oh, how I thanked our Lord this morning for allowing us to have this Leader and I asked God to keep him in His care and to give him all the blessings he so richly deserves! Look, I put a wreath of primroses, since nothing else is blooming yet, around his picture. AND I will make this a most festive day!" These last words were accompanied by a vigorous nod of her head and another tug on my braid.

Granny Becker's face was a sight to see. Her watery blue eyes almost rolled out of her wrinkled face. "But Mrs. Gutzeit, not mother Gutzeit as usual, how can you say such blasphemous things. To name that … that Hitler and God in one breath, and you, the most devout woman I know!"

"Mrs. Becker", came mother's deep and full voice again, "I want you to think for a moment and remember what we had the last three years, the riots, strikes, unemployment. The streets of Berlin and other cities were not safe! How often did Dorothea and Lisa have to wait for the mounted police to take them through the park to the school because of that child molester? Can't you see the changes brought about in those few months that Hitler is leading the country? I don't have to fear for the safety of the children, our papa has already had a pay raise and this after such a long wage freeze. And there are already more jobs available for the multitude of unemployed." Mother paused for a moment and pointed to the blue sky. "The weather is so beautiful, real Hitler weather. Is that not another sign that he is sent by God to help this bedraggled nation to get on its feet again?"

That last remark did it. Granny Becker limped hurriedly away, shaking her head so hard that she lost some hair pins from her thin gray bun. I jerked my head around to see whether mother had been struck by lightning or turned into stone for the sacrilegious things she had just said. All I got was a cuff on my ear with a "Hold still and let me finish your hair. You will be late for school and that will not do, not today, when you have a special assembly for our leader's birthday."

I got up slowly from my father's shoemaker stool, my head hurt- ing more than usual. The rough treatment of my hair was probably not intended and mother's anger over Granny Becker could account for it, but still every root of my hair felt like a hot needle. The brassy music from the radio, turned up to its full volume again, did not make things better.

My vivid memory of the day continues as I set off to meet with my sister, Lisa, waiting at the garden gate. With my school satchel on my back, my lunch box in hand, I said a meek good-bye to mother and joined my sister. We should have hurried as the unscheduled conversation with Granny Becker had taken up at least ten minutes of our thirty-minute walk to school. The sidewalk was not paved and I select- ed a piece of stone to kick around, a habit that I would only indulge in when I was perturbed and baffled. As my sister spoke "Don't, you will ruin your shoes," I exploded. "Dammit and to hell, you fat thing," I shouted as I stood with clenched hands behind my back or I would have hit her. "Do you have any feelings at all" I continued shouting. "You were staring at some imaginary castles in the clouds at the gate, while I had to listen to our mother making fun of God! I'll bet, you are not the least concerned whether she will be punished for that sin and maybe has to go to hell when she dies!"

My sister quickly answered "Don't worry, you will meet her there for the swear words you just said to me!"

I started to run and turned my head around so that the braids swung out on both sides and shouted "I don't even want to walk with you, you are so stupid!" As tears were stinging my eyes, I rubbed them with my fists, took a deep breath and said "Oh, come on you turtle, or we'll be late." She made two or three hurried steps and soon we fell into step again as we continued on to school, but neither of us spoke another word.

I knew that she pitied me for my short temper and many times in my life I berated myself; *Why, oh why, did I have my heart on my tongue?* I could almost see her pondering the fact that I was the elder sister and according to the rules of our home, I could command some measure of respect from my younger sister. But I often imagined that she must have thought, "life is so much easier, if you do what you should, what is expected, then wait; just wait, don't get excited or involved if you don't have to."

I was in turmoil. I often feared my stern mother, but also loved her with an intensity that almost hurt at times. I believed in my mother, hardly questioning anything she said or did. Sometimes if something was done or said that offended my sense of right or wrong,

I was always quick to find an explanation that absolved my mother from any wrongdoing. I would put it down as other people's faults, people who did not attend church as regularly as mother did and therefore could not live by the rules of the Bible. We children under- stood from earliest childhood that nothing and nobody could stand beside God the Almighty. All the creatures on earth, but especially people because they were given reason, were put on the earth to worship God. And this morning my mother put a man beside God! Such was the confusion in my mind, and so were the turmoil and emotions that were boiling in many households in Germany that year.

My headache was by now almost unbearable and with great effort I pushed these disturbing thoughts out of my mind. We were almost at the *Sud-schule* (south-school) when the big bronze bell rang signal- ing eight am, the start of school. We ran. With the last stroke of the bell the wide double doors, with Boys carved on top of one and Girls on the other, would be closed. Once the doors are closed the only way in would be to ring the bell at the smaller custodian's door and then we would have a red mark behind our names indicating that we were late. We just made it, sliding on the polished dark-brown linoleum floor to our class room. We flung our school bags on our seats and joined the other students lined up in the corridor ready to march into the gymnasium, which served as an auditorium as well.

This morning a special assembly was held to celebrate chancellor Hitler's birthday, his first since he came into office. All sports equipment was pushed against the walls and long rows of backless wooden benches were set up. These were slowly filling up with students of all grades. The portable stage was festively decorated with the old German flag, black, red and gold on one side and on the opposite side of the stage the new flag, red with the black swastika in a white circle. In the middle of the stage was a picture of Hitler in his brown storm- trooper uniform. A beautiful wreath of early spring flowers surrounded the picture. The concert piano was pushed to the edge of the stage where our music teacher sat in readiness. The several hundred students offered a somewhat strange sight. On usual Monday morning assemblies the children were always dressed a little bit better than on ordinary school days, but this day there were some brown uniforms of the Hitler youth and a few girls of the senior grades wore the dark blue skirts, white blouses and black kerchiefs with the leather knot of the B.D.M., (*Bund Deutscher Maedchen*), the girl's section of the Hitler youth. We were all urged to wear, if at all possible, a dark skirt or trousers with white blouses or shirts. Most of the children looked as if they wore uniforms, with only a few in their Sunday finery.

The school week usually started with a Monday morning assembly where, after a short period of hymn singing and meditative thoughts, the theme for the week was announced. But at this morning's assembly, as soon as the teaching staff came in solemn-faced and in dark suits, all the children rose as one body and our right arms went up in the Hitler salute. It is the same salute the Roman legionnaires used when they marched past the senators into battle with Germanic, Gaul and Briton tribes over 2,000 years ago. The music teacher intoned the national anthem, immediately followed with the famous tune and lyrics of "Germany, Germany, well beloved". For the first time in my life I sang with the others. This song had become the official Nazi Party song and was now the second official anthem of the Third Reich. A short translation gives an inkling of the power of the song's words:

Raise high the flags, stand rank on rank together,
Storm troopers march with steady quiet tread,
Comrades killed by communists and others,
In spirit march in our ranks with us.

Various teachers gave a few speeches, senior students recited appropriate poems and our mixed school choir, winner of many choir competition prizes, sang the magnificent Lutheran choral, "A mighty fortress is our God". This assembly had an electrifying atmosphere and for me this Lutheran hymn gave a moment of great elation.

When our principal, Rector Schultz, came to the lectern for the first time during this gathering, it was to lead us in the Lord's Prayer. Invariably it was said by him at the end of every school assembly. Rector Schultz had hardly finished saying the "Amen" when a boy shouted "Why didn't you pray for our Leader? After all it is his birthday is it not?" For a moment the entire assembly hall was deadly quiet. All breathing and movement had stopped among the hundreds of young people. A hot wave was rising in my neck as I stared at Rector Schultz. *O lord, what will he do?*, went through my mind.

Very slowly Rector Schultz took off his nickel rimmed glasses. His blue eyes, large as saucers, stared out over the audience. His face was an ashen white. Then with a voice I had never heard before, he thundered "You young fool! Did I not pray…and deliver us from evil!" His spectacles slipped through his fingers and he almost fell as he stormed down the few stage steps and out into the hallway. The heavy gymnasium door slammed behind him making the grand piano sing out a discordant note.

For a few seconds everyone was stunned. Then all hell broke loose. There was shouting, fist fights and girls screaming. The majority of the children, mostly the young ones, scrambled for the doors and in their haste pushed, shoved and fell. Our two male teachers, sport instructors, were shouting orders and trying to separate the fighting boys. It seemed to take forever to restore some kind of order and get the students back into their classrooms.

I was terrified by the sudden violence that shattered the serenity of the foregoing hour and by the outburst of Rector Schultz, which I could not really understand. I grant that the student was unruly in his manner of request to pray for Hitler. But why was Rector Schultz in such a rage? I had heard him saying prayers for President Von Hindenburg and surely would not Chancellor Hitler, appointed a few months ago by the president, deserve a prayer as well, especially on his birthday?

There was not much listening or learning done that day. The boys who supposedly started the fight and broke the rules of discipline were sent home. Before they could head for home, some had to go to the first-aid station where our home economics teacher doubled her duties as nurse.

We all feared some unheard of punishment for the initiators of this disturbance, but nothing happened. Rector Schultz, from whom we expected at the very least a stern lecture, was not seen in the school for days. He had a semi-detached home at the school but he did not leave his home, and was not seen standing at his usual place by the circular hall in the mornings to see his students come in. History lessons given exclusively by him for the senior classes were also cancelled. And not one of the teachers mentioned the incident, not even when the fighting heroes with their bruises of all shapes and colors came back to school.

However when the following week ended the official school year, Rector Schultz was there. A thinner and greyer Rector handed out the scholarships and awards. We thought for sure that he would say something then, but nothing was mentioned. There had been a teacher's conference the day before but no one spoke of it and nothing of what might have been said behind the closed conference room doors leaked out.

There was a custom among us children to have a small book, a *poesy* album, in which we asked special people on special occasions to write a verse or thought. I had a beautiful one, given to me by my father on my twelfth birthday a month before. It was bound in red Moroccan leather and had a lock with the tiniest of keys which I hung on a black velvet ribbon around my neck; it was the only adornment my mother allowed me to wear. At the school year end, all my form teachers had written something in it and my favorite fellow students too. Some had put worthwhile things in it, some silly little rhymes. It was a big thing to get Rector Schultz to write in one's poesy book. So on our last school day, not quite sure of myself or the reception I would get, I knocked on the Rector's study door. When I walked in ever so hesitantly, he impatiently waived his old spectacles, mended with an elastic band after they had suffered a fall on that fateful morning. To his, "Come in, come in, what do you want?" I answered in an almost inaudible voice and asked him to write some- thing in my album.

He motioned to a high-backed chair, called the "poor-sinner's chair" by the students because this is where one had to sit when a reprimand by the highest authority in the school was necessary. I sat on the edge and fumbled for the key, not taking my eyes off his face. There was a stained-glass window behind the rector that depicted a scholar in medieval robes raising a warning finger to the pupil before him, a very appropriate picture for an occupant of the poor sinner's chair facing it. Rector Schultz leaned back in his heavy leather captain chair and his head came into the path of a stream of sunlight. All of a sudden Rector Schultz's stern face was not frighten- ing any more. There was a warm smile around his thin lips, a twinkle in his eye and the iron grey hair with the brush-cut no longer looked comical to me. At that moment I did not realize that what I had seen in the old man's countenance was the beauty of a great soul.

He reached over, took my red album, selected a page and began to write. While his old-fashioned pen dipped in and out of the ink well, he spoke slowly the words he wrote: "BE TRUE AND SERVE". After a pause he added, "Frederick the Great".

"Thea". I winced at the shortening of my name. "Thea, I want you to listen very carefully and try to remember every word I am going to say to you now." As his face became serious and familiar again, my whole attention was geared to listen. "I have known your parents for a long time, and I like and respect them. They are pillars of our small Lutheran church, admirably dedicated, but at the same time they are also supporters of the New Order. They went through many hardships, disappointments and failures, and it is understandable that they believe the new regime, which began with Hitler's chancellery, will be for the good of our country. But, in the end it will not be so. Our future will be, to say the least, very, very trying. I suspect that you, with your logical and probing mind, will before long begin to question the integrity of the people who lend their support to this regime.

"Soon you will have to decide for yourself which stand you will take. If your convictions bring you in conflict with your parent's and other's convictions, never, never forget that your parents and the majority of people will act only on their strong beliefs of what is right at that particular time, in particular circumstances. Never lose sight of this fact when you are tempted to pass harsh judgment. The time will come when you can be of comfort and help to your parents, who love you and our fatherland. Prepare yourself for that time. Always be true to yourself, do right and be afraid of no one."

He said no more. I gathered my album and tiptoed to the door. I was just about to turn the knob when he called out and wagged a finger at me, "now you won't forget to laugh once in a while, life is great. Obstacles and difficulties are merely there to be overcome and believe me, that's done a lot more easily with a smile on your face and a laugh in your heart. Now go and enjoy your holidays."

When we came back for the new term one of the senior teachers had advanced to the post of principal and Rector Schultz, as he was still addressed, spent most of the day in the library advising us as to which book would be most suitable for this or that project. If the board of education, or whoever was responsible for his semi-retirement, had hoped to limit his influence on us students, their efforts were completely wasted. We went to the library during recess and after school and the Rector gave us all the time we wanted. We talked about everything under the sun and our Rector used this rare opportunity wisely. He influenced many students without us realizing it at the time; building a sort of mental balance-wheel in our minds, ready to swing into action at the slightest touch to counter-act many of the cynical attacks on reason, intelligence, and normal human behavior and emotions launched by the Regime-Orientation program of the New Regime.

By the end of that year Rector Schultz's full and forced retirement was announced and he dropped out of sight.

It was many years later before I fully understood the relationship between the incident at that special assembly in April of 1933, and his early retirement. After the Second World War was over, an honor detachment of the occupation forces along with hundreds of Berliners, I among them already the mother of two children, followed his funeral cortege to the cemetery and learned of his fate as it became public knowledge. An investigation triggered by his remarks during that school assembly resulted in imprisonment in a detention camp for his contradictory views regarding the Nazi government policies and for his close connections with the Socialist Party. During his imprisonment he wrote essays on child psychology and education. By the time of his death he was hailed as a modern Pestalozzi. (Pestalozzi 1770-1827 was a Swiss educator famous for his reforms in matters of education). I wept at his grave, and finally understood what he was trying to make me understand when he spoke so urgently to me that morning as he wrote in my poesy album "BE TRUE AND SERVE"

Before Rector Schultz was forced into his retirement, I had the benefit of his priceless lessons on history. In my final year at the South School, I enjoyed his special lectures, which he called 'Science of Life'.

It was during these lessons that he tried to engrave in our minds a very special sense of values with emphasis not on material matters but on basic rights and duties. Over and over again he urged us to be true to ourselves. If you have the least doubt about the rightness of what you are about to do or say, stop…think. Scrutinize your motives, because if you are intentionally malicious, rude or untrue to others, you will make them uncomfortable, hurt them, but the real damage is done to yourself! Whether you realize it or not, your conscience cannot be silenced and one a day in this life or another, you will be presented with the bill.

'Do not do unto others what you do not wish done to yourself'. This went through his lectures like a golden thread and took root in the students who listened. Later in my adult life, when the sense of values in most of us was warped by the horrible havoc brought by the war, I was more than once stopped from doing or saying something because I heard Rector Schultz's old voice saying "BE TRUE".

Hitler's chancellorship in 1933 brought radical changes that swept over Germany. The one that affected us youngsters immediately was that every boy or girl at the age of 10 had to become a member of the Hitler-Youth. My sister Lisa, who was 10 years old on January 3rd, had to join the girls section of the Hitler-Youth the *Bund Deutscher Maedchen*. There was no provision made for the older girls, so I got away without joining. My sister urged me to come to one of their meetings and see what it was like. So I went a few times. But what I saw and heard did not impress me. Everything was done with military precision, from marching around with a wimple (a small tri- cornered flag) carried in front, to singing marching songs, reciting slogans in unison: "Common interest before self" or even "Guns before butter". After a few visits with this group I decided this was not for me and never again went back to their functions. Lisa had to stay with them and attend all functions and lectures. The lectures were given under the motto "Blood and Honor". The German or Aryan race was proclaimed as superior and to keep the German race pure was made one of the main concerns for the youngsters. No mixing with inferior races, like Jews, Polish or Slavic people and keeping to a healthy life style was expected. No smoking, no make-up, and keeping fit was encouraged. In time the girls received some training in first aid and went camping generally having a good time. The whole concept was to indoctrinate the youngsters with National-Socialist ideas. It was done so subtly and cleverly that they were brainwashed for life without realizing it.

The youngsters had to stay in the Hitler-Youth or *Bund Deutscher Maedchen* until age 18 and most became so indoctrinated that they joined and became members of the National Socialist Party,

N.S.D.A.P. (National Socialist *Deutche Arbeiter* Workers Party). Lisa became an idealistic Party member and volunteered for all sorts of things. After the war ended she had to pay a bitter price for that. She was banned from gainful employment for a lengthy period of time and had to attend re-educational lectures. Then to erase her past as Party member, she had to perform the lowest and most menial tasks imaginable after which she was examined and declared "Nazi-free". Those were two hard and bitter years for Lisa. But during this time she found her religion again and in time became an active and enthusiastic Church member of the Lutheran church. I described Lisa's experience in some detail to show what I avoided by not having to become a member of the *Bund Deutscher Maedchen* or the "Party".

For me, the first inkling of what it meant to have a Nazi regime came in the late spring of 1934. Not far from our home was the former Cadet School, a compound for the SS Leibstandarte Adolf Hitler (a special regiment of the SS Schutzstaffel or bodyguard for Adolf Hitler.) In June 1934 there were shots ringing out from the cadet school. Men were executed all day long. A few days before there had been notices in the news papers that Ernst Roehm, head of the S.A. (Brownshirts) was in revolt against Adolf Hitler; the men around him were also implicated in this revolt. They were imprisoned and supposedly awaiting trial. A later rumor had it that Roehm and his friends were homosexual and that was also something that the Nazi's would not tolerate. This execution was the first time that the terror of the Nazi regime surfaced.

But I was only 14 and as yet relatively unaffected by the bitter tensions brewing in Germany. My youthful ignorance was more disturbed by the birth of my youngest sister Carin in September 1935. I was a bit embarrassed about this event. My mother was 44 years old and I felt she was much too old for another baby! But it didn't take long and my baby sister soon won my heart.

But before I go on further, I should mention something to clarify Hitler's position in Germany. When President von Hindenburg appoint- ed Hitler as chancellor in 1933 it was in accordance with the German constitution. Shortly thereafter Hindenburg died and Hitler immediately seized the opportunity to declare that the presidency and chancellorship would be combined. He took on both offices; from that time on he was generally known as *Fuehrer* (the Leader).

He became a dictator who imposed his will through weapons and violence as a public warning. Great bonfires grew in city squares during 1933, where books by Kafka or Brecht, Thomas Mann and Freud and others, whose writings the Nazi's termed *Kitsch*, or those written by Jews, were taken from bookstores and libraries and then publicly burned. Many artists, scientists and authors, such as Einstein, Freud, Brecht and Marlene Dietrich were able to leave Germany ahead of the great purge; often there was help from outside Germany to accomplish their defection. Sometimes, businessmen especially were able to buy their freedom from the Nazis. These acts outraged even my parents; although they endorsed many aspects of Hitler's regime, because this regime had brought Germany out of the depression and anarchy that were the legacies of the First World War. Even they were aghast at the book burning, the expropriation and disappearance of paintings by non-Aryan, and the intolerance against Jewish and non-Aryan peoples. Thankfully our family was not directly involved in or affected by these things. Many of Hitler's atrocities, like the hideous concentration camps, came to light only after the war was over. What was known, for instance, was that criminals, people opposed to Nazi ideology, and communists were put into labor camps, together with Jews, and made to work in factories important for the war effort. The war effort, leading to the Second World War, was propelled forward as Hitler realized that Germany required more raw materials than Germany could provide, as the Treaty of Versailles disallowed Germany to trade with other countries. To solve this, he would simply invade another country and obtain their raw materials; and his actions would further his cause.

Just a few years later I was to work in one of those factories, the Spinnstoffabrik, where rayon and staple fibers were produced and used to make uniforms for the *Wehrmach* (army). From my office window I could observe the arrival of columns of people in their black and white striped clothes with different colored insignia or bars on the shoulders. These shoulder markings identified Communists or any person opposed to Hitler's regime, including Jews, and other religious such as Jesuits and in fact, any pastor of any denomination opposing the regime, as well as ordinary criminals. The existence of the concentration camps and the extermination camps was kept so secret that even the people in whose district they were located did not know about them. Naturally, during the latter war years, rumors circulated but were quickly put out of mind as completely impossible!

Anti-Jewish slogans began to appear as frequent as street signs, disappearing for a short time only, during the 1936 Olympic games held in Berlin. All of Berlin was decked out in the flags of the participating nations. There was a festive feeling in the city and with the recently mounting tensions anxiously relieved, everyone seemed to be everyone's friend. The Olympic stadium and Olympic village that housed the athletes were something to behold in their architectural beauty. But there was a silent laugh throughout Germany when Jesse Owens, and American black, won a gold medal and Hitler had to stand up during the playing of the American anthem in honor of Jesse's victory. According to Nazi ideology, Blacks in addition to Slavic, Polish, and Jewish persons, were considered inferior to the "pure" German and Aryan race.

During the Olympic games lodging was at a premium in Berlin and my parents were quick to seize the opportunity. Every room in our house was rented to visitors and my sisters and I slept on canvas folding lawn chair-loungers in the living room. Although sleeping was uncomfortable we had great fun. We savored every word our visitors had to tell us about the Olympic Games. But after the games every- thing in Berlin went back to a somber normal. Jews once again were obliged to wear a patch with the yellow star of David sewn on their clothing and anti-Jewish slogans sprouted everywhere once again. Now the anti-Jewish movement escalated with a further obstacle thrown in their way when a general boycott was declared against anything Jewish.

As I had not much personal experience with the dark side of Nazi politics and was only minimally interested in politics at all, my young life was happy. I enjoyed continuing my education with two years in the business college. The teachers taught interesting and diverse subjects; I was once again in my element, reading and studying. But in 1937, at the ripe age of sixteen, after finishing business college I found, with the help of my father, a position in the Spinnstofffabrik Zehlendorf (rayon and nylon factory) *Spinnstoff* roughly translated means fiber from a spinning wheel, however a *Spinne* is also a spider, hence the factory soon had the nickname the *Spinne* (the Spider). I was excited to launch my life in a business career though I always aspired to continue studies at university, but there were many periods of layoff and interruptions caused by the political and economical climate and war. I continued to work there on-and-off for nearly eighteen years until 1955.

Life during the tender years that pass between the teenage years and young adulthood was great! School was completed for now although never relinquishing my aspirations to continue on to University, I decided to enjoy my career. I put my efforts into the job with the *Spinne* and spent time on *Sportsplatz* which I loved. On the week-ends there were trips to compete in track and field in other cities. Thus my life was busy and full. At the *Spinne* I soon became recreational sports director, and my life felt full of promise. With the Nazi belief that "only in a healthy body, lives a healthy mind", most workplaces had a time and place set aside for exercise. To make my life complete, after work, our home provided the ample companionship of a large family. There was always action, excitement, and fun with my sisters, as Lisa who was also maturing contributed stimulating conversation and arguments. Christa, with her youthful and fun loving attitude, could smooth out the most difficult discussions. And of course there was my baby sister Carin. Mother, although stern and religious, did have wonderful teas and garden socials which, although boring at times, provided delightfully delicious sweets. I adored my father and the many philosophical talks he and I had. This completed the picture of my terrific adolescent period.

I was sixteen and was just getting into the groove with my new job and life when my world and dreams were shattered. My father was tragically killed in a train accident. I'm not sure how it was decided who would come from the train station, where my father was stationmaster, to inform my mother "The woman with all those children". Devastated and in shock, we were all stunned. My mother was left with four children of her own, the youngest, Carin, only two years old, and my young cousin Gerd to bring up. My father's full pension was not to be realized as he had not quite completed his papers for promotion. My mother was left with a difficult situation and hard times ahead of her.

Any dreams I had about still being able to go to a university and study journalism were finished. I was the oldest of the children, and my sister, Lisa, two years younger than I, had just started business school, so my job at the *Spinne* would provide the family income. My sister Christa and cousin Gerd were still at the *Sud Schule*. My whole salary went to the family fund and I kept only a minimal sum for pocket money.

I buried my sorrow with exercise and my commitment to the position of Ladies sports director at the *Spinne*. Before long I became friends with the sports director of the men's division. We talked and enjoyed a comradeship in sports, but more than that, our friendship developed to include a three-week kayak trip across the waterways of Germany. The collapsible kayak and our backpacks carried us through sunshine and rain as we paddled through Pomerania and Mecklenburg via the chain of lakes and the river Elbe to Hamburg. Although our friendship was close it could not compensate for the loss of my father, and I was not ready for a relationship. But the adventure did teach me how to repair torn canvas, bear the muscle fatigue and strain of heavy paddling, and show me a Germany made more beautiful when viewed from the waterways. I will never forget our anxious excitement as we accidentally found ourselves in the middle of a busy commercial harbor, furiously paddling in the wake of the huge ocean liners.

Our family was busy with itself and so we were oblivious to the happenings of the political scene. The *Anschluss*, the annexation of Austria in the spring of 1938 and the occupation of the Sudetenland, part of Czechoslovakia, were events both applauded in Germany and by the majority of the people. But there were ominous signs fore- telling disaster such as the ramping up of arms and ammunition production, the swift completion of the Autobahn (highway) and the finishing of the west wall on the border to France. The production of the Volkswagen and *Volksempfaenger* (small radio) was stepped up as Hitler wanted to make it possible for every household to have an inexpensive radio. All this brought the unemployment rate down to almost zero. The depression of the early thirties was not forgotten, and the population was happy with everyone employed. Not even the occupation of the Sudetenland brought the thought of an impending war nearer. But those who were awake to all these signs hoped right up to the last minute that war could be avoided.

Then, in early September of 1939, the German army marched into Poland, and the brutal truth became evident to my family. There was no explanation or excuse for this. Austria and the Sudetenland were explained by claiming that these areas were of German roots with German spoken there. The non-aggression pact signed with the Soviet union was a ray of hope. But then the persecution of the Jews was stepped up heading to the infamous *Kristallnacht* with the destruction of Jewish houses, business and synagogues. Along with the Anti Jewish slogans, war slogans were appearing, such as *Erst Waffen dann Butter* (arms before butter).

As we lived on the outskirts of Berlin we had very little contact with the city and what happened there came usually as a rumor, by word-of-mouth, and only sometimes in newspapers or over the radio. However it was via the radio that we heard about the *Kristallnacht* when the S.A. (Brownshirts) 'cleansed' the city of Jews. What happened on crystal-night is now a well known event in history. During that night, Nov 9, 1938, every known Jewish business was ransacked and destroyed with display windows smashed (hence the name 'crystal-night') Jews were literally dragged out of their homes, beaten and imprisoned, and many were killed as a prelude of the horrors yet to come. Placards appeared overnight with the slogan *Jews raus* (Jews out) And the hunt for Jews was on.

It was about this same time that I found myself bored with my work in the purchasing department of the *Spinne*. The monotony of my work and with the compulsory enlistment term of half a year in an *Arbeitsdienst* (compulsory voluntary work term for your country) looming over me, as I was yet obligated to complete my half year, made the time right for me to enlist. With the thought of escaping and thinking that I wanted to see something of the world, I enlisted for the regular term of half a year in the *Arbeitsdienst*, an organization that took young male and females to help primarily with the farmers. It should be noted that the male division had some military training as well. After a thorough medical examination I was accepted and sent to Lipke, a small village on the Polish border.

We lived in cold and drafty barracks. But the warmth of the comradery that developed among the young women who shared the bunk-house made the difficult work and harsh environment tolerable. We even managed to have fun, but the work detail was rigorous both at the camp and out. Of course we had to take turns with kitchen and general housekeeping duties but our main occupation was helping the farmers. As we learned to do all the things that had to be done, memories of my grandfathers farm flooded back, but now I no longer viewed the labors as a dreamy childhood pastime. There was a real and sincere closeness that was coupled with the light-heartedness of the girls in the barracks who were all roughly the same age.

Because this farming village was very close to German occupied Poland, a detachment of eleven men from the *Arbeitsdienst* were living in a separate barrack with orders to look after our safety. Herbert Stimming, my future husband, was one of those men. We fell madly in love and despite the enforced discipline, we found time and chance for courtship.

THREE

1939 - 1945

The war years and Herbert

I know very little of Herbert's ancestors and the Stimming family, but I do know that at one time in their history they must have distinguished themselves in public service and became wealthy enough to receive a family crest. To become the bearer of a family crest was quite an honor which was bestowed on very few people. The motto chosen on this heralding crest *Rump hart clat Stimming* indicates that some of the earlier Stimmings might have been sea-faring people. The motto is Early Modern German which was spoken about 300 to 400 hundred years ago and the meaning of which, roughly translated means, to "Hold fast, sail clear".

I met Otto, the patriarch of the Stimming family and grandfather of Herbert, for the first time in 1941 just before my wedding. Otto was a sturdy gentleman of middle height with a white brush cut. Otto owned and operated a dairy business, including delivery to retail and grocery stores. He had land in the Uckermark, a part of the County of Brandenburg which surrounds Berlin. There he kept his dairy herd. The milk was sent from there in large milk cans by rail to Berlin. Then in the early morning hours, around 2:00 am, the trucks were loaded with the milk cans for delivery to the retail and grocery stores. Otto did not handle any of this personally as he had many employees. However on rare occasions he would supervise the un- loading in Berlin. His dairy business had been large and prosperous, but now it was also suffering from the effects and restrictions that the beginning of the war was imposing.

He had built a large house in Berlin Pankow on Schloss Strasse, in the North-west corner of the city. The house contained four apartments, two on the first floor and two on the second. His son Wilhelm, Herbert's father, lived with his family in one of the second-floor apartments which was across the hall from Otto. Attached to this house was a large garage which housed mostly trucks, but I can remember that there was a Desoto car on blocks as during the war there was no gas allowed for private use. The Stimmings also owned other houses that were rented out, as well as the two apartments on the first floor of the main house which now also had renters in them.

Otto had a daughter late in life, Kaethe, who was born in 1921, the same year as Otto's grandson Herbert was born. She later married her first cousin and they had a son, Bernd. Bernd is about the same age as my son Rainer. As far as I know, Bernd is still living in Berlin as I write these Stimming memories in 1999, and he probably operates what is left of the dairy business. But who looked after the dairy business right after Otto died is not clear to me. His son Wilhelm, Herbert's father, worked for a bank. Later, after the war, Kaethe and her husband took over the remnants of the dairy business and made a go of it. Herbert had refused when it was offered to him in 1945. Although the war was over and jobs were scarce, the idea of getting up in the middle of the night to arrange and supervise the unloading of the milk just did not appeal to Herbert. Constant supervision and hard work are major requirements to rebuild any business, and especially so during that time of disarray and confusion that was the legacy of World War II. And that is how I come to assume that Kaethe's son Bernd would have continued to run what was left of it in later years.

To understand more about Otto's dairy business, it must be understood that when I met Herbert's family at the beginning of World War II, Otto was already semi-retired from the business. And after the war the land in Uckermark was still owned by Herbert's family when Berlin became an "island city" in the Russian occupation zone of Germany. Uckermark was in that Russian zone. After the war special papers with appropriate authorization were required to travel from the Russian zone to West Germany. Even more authorization and papers were required to do business. The island city of Berlin was even further divided into four sectors: Russian, American, British and French. The American, British and French sectors in the west and north-west of Berlin began to be generally known as West Berlin. The Russian sector in the east half of Berlin, soon became known as East Berlin. Then a few years later it was even necessary to have special permission to travel from West to East within Berlin.

If one needed to go out of West Berlin and travel to the West-zone of Germany one required not just all the special papers and permission, but lots of time and patience. The many checkpoints en route via the corridor through East Germany, or the DDR (Deutsche Democratic Republic) as it became known, was staffed with eager Soviet security patrols who seemed to enjoy detaining everyone for as long as possible. It was difficult enough to do business during the war, but after the war, with the division of Germany, followed by the division of Berlin, it was a nightmare.

For a few years, until the Russians closed off any access by land to West Berlin, the dairy business went on as usual, even with the difficulties of constantly renewing the access papers and the time-consuming and aggravating checkpoints. Then access by land was closed off and milk was brought to Berlin from West Germany, also by special permission. I do not know what happened during all this time to the land in Uchermark, in East Germany. Mention of it surfaced for the first time nearly 50 years later in 1999, ten years after West and East Germany was reunited after the fall of the Berlin Wall. A search was conducted for the heirs to the land; I assume to collect 50 years of retroactive payments.

I'm getting ahead of my story. I think back to when Herbert and I met, just before the war, while stationed at adjoining work camps. It was fun to sneak to our secret meetings. We may have fooled the officers, but not our comrades, who were supportive of our affair. Love is persistent and even though our time together was restricted by distance and commitments, Herbert's and my romance flourished after we left the *Arbeitsdienst* camp. Our love affair became serious and Herbert decided to take me to meet his family. Otto's wife and Herbert's grandmother, Helene, liked me at first sight, and when I was introduced to her in 1941, she spontaneously took off a ring from her hand and gave it to me. Flattered and proud, I wore this three-diamond ring with its antique setting for many years, until I passed it to my daughter Monika for safe-keeping for in turn to give to my son Rainer's adult son's wife after I was gone. By then the ring would have been worn through five generations, making this beautiful ring an heirloom, I would think!

Wilhelm Stimming, Herbert's father, was a banker, more reserved in character than the strong, outgoing character of his father Otto. The banking business suited him well. At that time the German banks had an entirely different set-up from the banks here today. All cash in the bank was handled by one person, the cashier. Customers would state their business to the teller who handed over the necessary documents along with a number to the cashier. The customers took a seat until they were called by the cashier who would then complete the withdrawal or deposit. The position of cashier was held in high esteem and always by a man; an honorable and well paid position it ranked with that of bank manager. Wilhelm was proud of his career as cashier. But to his greater benefit, his income was supplemented further by the dividends from the dairy business, as well as a part of the rental income of the apartments and huge garage that was attached to the Stimming's family home. Herbert's family had substantial finances and status.

Herbert's mother, Wilhelm's wife, was named Else and later known to my children as "Pankowoma". I was excited and flattered to be invited to meet my future parents-in-law Wilhelm and Else Stimming. Along with Herbert, they had two more children: Werner, who was killed at the Russian front during WWII in the Baltic Provinces, and Erika, who married in 1948. Tragedy came to the family again when Erika died of leukemia in 1956. I must stop my story to mention Else's father, Wilhelm Keller, who died in WWI and Else's mother, Elizabeth. I mention Elizabeth because my great grandson looks exactly like her with his narrow face and his slim figure.

I think it is time to turn my memories back to Herbert and the love affair that began at the *Arbeitsdienst* camp in October 1939. Our romance began with the zest of youth, the excitement of camp and the anxious foreboding of war. For my "compulsory" "voluntary" *Arbeitsdienst*, I volunteered for the organization formed by Hitler to assist farmers, especially during harvest time. *Arbeitsdienst* was also viewed by Hitler as a means to keep young men and women occupied between those years of school, apprenticeship and a job. Work was tiring and labor-intensive, but the farmers treated us with hospitality and warmth as our help was welcomed. Aside from the camp comrade- ship and the fun that a whole group of same-aged girls can have when working together, work and life in the camp was demanding. I remember the barrack buildings where we slept as being nothing more than flimsy wooden buildings, with no insulation and of course no inside toilets. We were always cold.

Along with the farm work, the girls received first-aid training, but the boys were given priority in military training. The Lipke camp, close to the military front at the Polish border was dangerous. The boys, at the camp stationed close by, took their job of protecting the girls seriously, but none more than Herbert as he charmed us girls and held his weapon and demeanor with pride. It was easy to fall in love with him. With his blonde good looks he was the "golden boy" among the young men.

We both fell in love at first sight. The discipline of camp life with forty young women in it was in itself restrictive. But Herbert and I found time to be together and allow our affair to flourish. All through that winter the glow of romance kept us warm and happy. But in April of 1940 Herbert transferred to the military, to a mounted artillery regiment, while I went back to Berlin-Zehlendorf. Our six months of *Arbeitsdienst* was finished.

Herbert's regiment was stationed in Kuestrin, about 140 km east of Berlin. (After the second world war, Kuestrin was given to Poland along with all the land east of the Oder River.) During the first two years after we met, in the early years of the war, travel was not too restricted and every chance I had I would go via train to Kuestrin. Even after he was stationed at different cities across Germany, and as long as it was possible, I would visit him as often as I could. I traveled to Naumburg, Bad Kosen, Braunschweig and Leipzig. Later, once Germany occupied France, he was transferred there. It was courtship by distance. Sometimes it was not easy to get time off from work, but I managed.

When I came back from the *Arbeitsdienst* in April 1940, still dream- ing of becoming a journalist, I tried to find a job with a newspaper, without luck. So when the *Spinne* contacted me to come back to work, I went. But I would always scrounge to have days off to make these frequent trips to see my Herbert. During my time with the *Spinne*, I worked in various departments (bookkeeping, invoice control, research) and all of it was more interesting than the purchasing department where I had begun and become so bored.

There were many visits to the different places where Herbert was stationed, but the trip I remember as the most difficult was when I travelled from Berlin to Breslau in Upper Silesia, now also in Poland. Upper Silesia was the staging point for the assault on Stalingrad and was overrun with soldiers. From here, Herbert's unit was to advance to Stalingrad and the important battle raging there. I had to convince my employers, the train bureaucrats, my mother, but most of all myself that I should go. Thankfully, the trip itself was uneventful, but the train ride was long and grueling as it stopped often to pick up soldiers to be taken to the front. The atmosphere in the train was always tense and after another long ride back, I was relieved to reach home again.

This battle around Stalingrad would be called the decisive battle in the war with Russia, the second front. The first front was in Western Europe and it was raging, especially the *Luftkreig* air battle over England. But in Stalingrad it was the Russian ground troops that completely surrounded the German troops. The Russian troops relentlessly hammered away at the many German army corps fighting there. The siege took many weeks, and the Russian grip on the German soldiers was firm. The generals of the enclosed German army petitioned Hitler to send the Luftwaffe to help get the soldiers out of that enclosed Russian city; but Hitler refused an airlift and gave orders to hold out in Stalingrad. Literally tens of thousands of German and Russian men died, and many German soldiers were taken prisoner-of-war by the Russians. The battle of Stalingrad became a total disaster for Germany and the beginning of the end of the German Army on the eastern front.

But Herbert was lucky. Early in the battle of Stalingrad he became ill and was sent back to Germany. He was one of the few who escaped the annihilation of the largest assembly of German forces. He had a gallbladder infection and was in a field hospital in Bad Cozen, a lovely area in the middle of Germany. It was possible for me to visit him in the hospital there. After his convalescence, he was stationed for many months in Germany, away from the raging battle fronts. Even with battles raging, it now became possible for our courtship to flourish; I met his family and wedding plans were made.

All through my teenage years I was very active in track-and-field sports, and cycled at least twice a week to the *Sportsplatz* spending many energetic hours there, and I was often a competitor at competitions. A few days before my wedding day I was waiting my turn in a shot put event and was playing with the heavy balls, tossing them over my head from one hand to the other, back and forth, when the ball slipped. It smashed into my mouth knocking out part of my two front teeth. In pain and humiliated I did not allow a single wedding picture to be taken with me smiling.

Herbert was given only three days wedding leave and we were married on October 24th, 1942. I have to tell a bit about the marriage laws of Germany. The couple had first to be married before a registrar for a "civil ceremony". A church wedding, having no legal bearing, was like the icing on a cake. Those couples who could afford it had a church wedding the day after the civil one. This meant that the bride could have two separate outfits, an elegant one for the civil ceremony and the white wedding finery for the church wedding. Even though Germany was on ration cards by this time, my family together had enough clothing ration card points that I could wear a very nice dress suit with matching hat for the civil wedding. My beautiful white wedding dress was created from many sources. My mother had a girlfriend in East Prussia who was a dressmaker; Mother promised her a large portion of our fruit harvest from our garden in return for her sewing. The girlfriend, who also raised poultry, exchanged a goose for material and made the dress for me. I never had a chance to try it on beforehand, but it fit perfectly! With Herbert's mother lending me her bridal veil, my outfit was complete.

Sadly, there was no church wedding after all. German civilians were now facing restrictions with transportation and travel, and a church wedding would simply be too complicated for everyone. So my mother arranged to have the pastor come to our house. She decorated the living room with many sprays of flowers and ribbons which gave the room a festive setting appropriate for the occasion. The wedding guests sat on the rows of chairs neatly lined up and instead of organ music, Herbert's brother Werner played Richard Wagner's *Lohengrin* wedding march on the violin. Herbert, a better-than-average piano player, and his brother also provided the entertainment later in the evening. Although we were not well off, my parents insisted on music in the house and a piano had been added to the living room many, many years before. For my wedding feast, mother engaged the help of two ladies, who benefited from the left-over food. The whole affair, which later spilled over into the garden, was festive and great. I remember that this day, with the exception of the baptism of my first two children, was the last great occasion to celebrate for a very long time, for both the duration of the war and some time after.

Our wedding day in October of 1942, was an exceptionally warm and sunny day. I remember as we all sat in my mother's beautiful garden watching Otto, Herbert's grandfather, munching on apples. He looked so robust and healthy, showing no sign of the stomach cancer that would claim his life a year later.

In 1943 the war became intense in Berlin and was now at our garden gate. With constant air raids, travel of any kind became extremely difficult and being pregnant I stayed home. I had mixed feelings. Although I was ecstatic with the thought of having a baby, I was very scared about bringing a new life into these unsettled and chaotic times. By July 23, 1943 when Monika was born, the war had already taken an ugly turn and my travels were curtailed further, much to Herbert's annoyance. He was not stationed at a military front but instead still stationed in remote areas of Germany, quiet and away from the battles. He could not understand the travel challenges I faced. He became angry with me that my visits had stopped. The allied air force had started bombing German cities, especially Berlin, in earnest and he could not understand the fear and chaos I found myself in.

With German troops invading Russia it was clear, to most of us, that this was the beginning of the end for Germany as we knew it. Russia and Germany had signed a "non-aggression agreement" but Hitler broke that agreement without provocation when he ordered his troops to march into Russia. My mother cried when the broadcast news announced Germany's invasion into Russia. She knew Russia. She was stationed on the Russian front as a field nurse during WWI. She knew of the vast distances an army would have to cover and of the difficulties of getting supplies to the front. She knew the hardships the soldiers would face. We all remembered Napoleon's attempt to conquer Russia, which also ended in disaster. We knew Hitler's decision to invade Russia would end in failure, and break Germany.

Now Germany was engaged on all fronts and the nightly allied attacks on Berlin frayed our nerves. We were kept in a state of constant anxiety as we tried to manage our daily business of living. As I cuddled my baby, Monika, I silently worried about the world this terrible war would leave for her.

An acquaintance of ours had access to a hunting lodge about 60 km east of Berlin. She lived there with her baby son in order to be away from the relentless bombing of the city. She invited me to join her with baby Monika. I finally agreed to leave my family home and in January 1943 traveled to that hunting lodge. It was very remote, a one hour walk to the nearest grocery store and about that far again to the train station. It seemed quiet and peaceful but from here we could observe the bombing of Berlin as the whole night sky was alight with explosions and resulting fires. The battle of the two air forces and firing of the anti-air-craft weapons from the ground allowed those explosions to be seen at great distances, with lights pulsating over the city. One could almost feel the direct impact of the bombs, with the noise carrying as far as this remote hunting lodge. The tension and worry was worse than being in the middle of it all. So, after a couple of weeks, I went back to my family home in Berlin.

I managed one more trip to visit Herbert in Braunschweig early in January 1944. After my marriage I had continued to live at my mother's home and she offered to look after baby Monika for me. It was hard for me to leave my beautiful first-born daughter as I was thrilled to have her. From the moment she was born, I loved her immensely. But I took my heart into my hands and went alone by train to Braunschweig. The trip itself was difficult and my visit in Braunschweig odd, but it wasn't until much later in our married life that I would find out what a huge role Braunschweig would play in our marital relationship.

Life in Berlin was becoming more and more difficult, and I was pregnant again. On September 5, 1944 Rainer was born and Herbert managed a few days leave to visit me in the hospital. I had been ill and the pregnancy did not set well with me. The war, work, caring for my first born and doing my share at the house and garden all took its toll. By this time we spent most of the days and nights in the basement. I was so sick that I didn't care about much during the birth, but then I took one look at the scrawny baby boy and I loved him instantly. Glad as I was to see Herbert, I found it to be a strange meeting. Herbert, usually oblivious to other people's stress, was generally a happy-go-lucky and cheerful man. Not so at this visit. He was depressed and moody with a preoccupied mind that I could not understand until many months later.

By now the fronts of the allied armies had come ever so close to Berlin and the air raids were non-stop. Travel was completely out of the question as it was difficult enough just to go to the corner store, which, by the way, supplied little. The mail service was haphazard at best, often interrupted or non-existent. Letters between Herbert and me, even though he was still stationed in Germany, became almost impossible too. The last I heard was that he was sent to the southern part of Germany, to the Italian front.

When the air raids and bombs over Berlin intensified, we had many anxious moments. Even though we lived on the outskirts of Berlin and the heavy bombing was mostly in Berlin proper, some bombs fell close enough to shatter our windows. Inside our house we once found a non-activated (live) bomb in our laundry room. There was an old mattress stored upright, leaning against one wall. When we moved the mattress, we saw the bomb imbedded in it. Soon we no longer felt safe in the basement and decided to squeeze into the water meter closet when we heard the air raid sirens. This was a tiny, bunker-like square dug in our front garden and it had an iron lid. This little bunker was just large enough to house the water meter dial and allowed one man comfortable access to read it. We squeezed the whole family in there … all of us, often four or five adults with the two babies. My mother, sisters Lisa and Christa, (when she was still here in Berlin) little Carin and Gerd, myself and the babies and any other family member who happened to be visiting. We felt that a bomb would have to land directly on top of us to kill us and we would all go at once. And if a bomb landed nearby and buried us with earth, our neighbors would know where to look for us.

Across from our home and two properties down, just past the Telefunken headquarters, was a huge empty field. When I was very young it was a large wheat field, but now it was overgrown with scrubby grasses. Early in the war, anti-aircraft guns were stationed there and the German soldiers who operated them built a temporary bunker. This bunker was dug down and was half covered with earth. There was a generator for light but water had to come from elsewhere. Our house was the first they would come to after the two empty properties and it was to us that they came for water. Naturally, as this was a daily chore, we came to know the soldiers well. Some of their free time was spent in our home. We played chess, loaned them our books and sometimes they stayed for a home-cooked meal. When they were transferred we continued contact with them by mail as best we could. And long after the war was over, we continued correspondence with some of them and their families.

Right from the beginning of the war the enemy aircraft flew over Berlin to their targets in

Germany. And in the beginning, my sister Lisa and I, curious as young people are, would go outside when an air raid was on. Fascinated, we would watch the activity in the sky. One night when we were standing in the garden, eyes following the searchlights which had enemy aircraft in their beams, we heard the familiar *ack-ack-ack* of the anti-aircraft guns, but in between there were these strange smacking noises that we could not identify. Next day when our mother sent us out to the garden to get some cabbages, the smacking noises were explained. Sticking out of the cabbage heads were metal splinters of all sizes. We realized then how lucky we were that none of these splinters had fallen on us and pierced our head.

We were lucky in so many ways. There was destruction all around but our house lost only a few windows. We were lucky in other ways too. Early in 1940 the German ration cards for groceries, textiles, gas and cigarettes were organized. Again our family was fortunate as we had the large garden with vegetables and fruits. Our hens supplied eggs and meat. We could augment our meager ration card with pro- duce from our own garden and even had enough left to barter for other necessary goods. So it was that we were never hungry during the war … not until the end of it, in April 1945. By then ration cards were no longer of any use, as there was nothing to buy and April was not harvest time!

Even during the war with its misery, death and destruction, shortages and restrictions, there were some light moments, provided by the most unlikely source— hedgehogs. We had a family of them in our garden for some time. We were cultivating them because they were policing the bugs, grubs and insects harmful to our vegetables and flowers. Late one evening we noticed that they were on our front door step and appeared very agitated. A short time later the air raid sirens were blaring. That same sequence happened several nights. We reasoned that the animals must have heard or sensed the approaching enemy aircraft before the sirens could warn us humans. Soon it became a routine to check for the hedgehogs every evening. Later when the air raids occurred during the day as well, they were there on our door step warning us then too. We rewarded the faithful hedgehogs with the occasional dish of raw scrambled egg and milk that was precious for us, but their warnings were even more so.

The war raging on, yet by now we all knew the war was lost for Germany as we held our breath and watched the advance of the Russian troops from the East and the allied troops from the West. Many Germans, among them my sister Lisa, were convinced that Hitler had a 'Secret Weapon' with which he would hold the onslaught of troops. Life became more and more frantic. In the Fall of 1944 every bit of vegetable and fruit from our garden was preserved and put into the basement although this was to prove of no use for us at all.

With the telephone connections completely down and minimal communications available, I undertook a perilous journey right across Berlin to look for my parents-in-law. I was very worried about them as there was heavy fighting towards the end of the war in the Pankow district of Berlin where they lived. I was lucky that I could use the *Stadtbahn* (City train) at least part of the way, but mostly I walked through the bombed out and still smoking ruins. I was nervous and a fear bordering on panic gripped my very being. But fear had become a daily companion for everyone as we went about doing what was necessary to survive. After many hours when I finally came to the place where the Stimming house used to be, I found a burnt-out ruin. Neighbors told me that the Stimmings were alright and now lived in one of the other apartment houses they owned. I continued my journey as this apartment was not too far from there. I was relieved to find that both parents-in-law and my young sister-in-law,

Erika were alright. But what a story they told. The main house had survived the bombings and it was drunk Russian soldiers who destroyed the house by setting it on fire. In the hurried escape from the burning house, my mother-in-law Else and Erika managed only to salvage a bird in a cage where a small bag of their jewelry was hidden. I heard nothing of Herbert. After a short rest I set out once again through the smoldering streets of Berlin towards my home.

It was about this time that I became seriously ill with an acute appendix attack; it was decided that surgery was necessary. This was major surgery and while in the hospital, still in the first days of recovery, the news of the Russians invading Berlin loomed over me. The worry and fear for my children and family outweighed any logic. Time for recuperation was no longer a concern. Before the clamps that held the incision together could be removed, barely a few days after surgery, I got dressed, left the hospital and walked home. That it took months before I felt better is an understatement! Even with my diligent care and cleansing, it was weeks before the clamps worked themselves free.

At the end of April 1945, when we could already see the Russian tanks moving through our neighborhood I urged my mother, who was not well at the time, and my sisters to leave our house and seek shelter further into the city. I reasoned that there would be safety in numbers with the hoards of Berliners seeking refuge in the shelters. Both my mother and sister Lisa belonged to the Nazi party and were known as party members. I was afraid that neighbors would denounce the whole family as Nazis to the Russians, and there would be reprisals. After much convincing, we bundled the two children into the baby carriage, took as many valuables as we could carry, and struggling, pushing the carriage over the rubble, we walked together north-east to the center of Berlin.

It was high time that we left our home. In heated and hurried argument I urged my sister to remove the large poster of Hitler that she had placed on an easel, draped with swastika flag and surround- ed with a garland of early Spring flowers. The whole thing stood in front of our house in the garden. One can imagine the impact this would have had on the Russians! It was the 20th of April, Hitler's birthday, and my sister, totally captivated by Hitler and the new regime, had placed it there to honor the day with this exhibition! That we would be courting rape by the Russian soldiers and even death by staying home was certain … but this display was insanity! She relented and hurriedly removed it just as we left, with the Russians now at the top of our street.

After a walk of more than three hours we made it to some friends of my parents who lived in a huge apartment block in Steglitz, which was a district closer to the center of Berlin. There we found shelter in the basement with several hundred other people. We stayed in that basement, on straight-backed chairs for several days. Heavy bombardment and fighting was happening everywhere around us. Until one day when there was an ominous quiet and the basement door opened to allow some heavily-armed Russian soldiers in. With pointed weapons they walked among us and demanded *uri, uri* (watch in German is *uhr*). They wanted watches, jewels and anything else that they could carry. Early in May of 1945 Berlin fell and was occupied by the Russian army. A terrible time lay ahead for the conquered Berliners.

We waited almost a week, and then my mother decided to take my youngest sister Carin and walk back to check on our house. Two days later they returned to tell us our house was still there, but in complete shambles. Deciding to go back, we trekked through the smoldering ruins and the remnants of the street fighting back to our house. Luckily it still stood. But what a shock. A group of mounted Russian soldiers had occupied our house and destroyed everything! The garden was completely trampled. In the house, preserves were smashed and mixed with clothing, upholstery torn from the couch and chairs, bedding slashed, feces smeared on the walls and every- thing that could be of use was stolen. But there was a silver lining. A sack of oats, probably for the horses, became a lifeline for myself and the baby Rainer. Just a baby, he needed a bottle. As there was nothing to feed him, I ground the oats in the coffee grinder, mixed it with water and pressed it through a sieve. This I put into his bottle. Thankfully both of the babies thrived on the diet of horse oats as the pictures of that time show. They almost looked too fat and healthy, but it was just from the horse oats and I'm grateful to have had that to give to them.

We were visited by Russian soldiers almost daily who demanded food and all sorts of goods. We gave them what we had, and soon found that when they saw we had babies, they became friendlier and less demanding. I made sure the babies were always visible.

It was almost June before it was possible to get milk for the children. I had to walk daily for over an hour to a farmer on the out- skirts of the city to get a pitcher of milk. On the way I was often stopped by patrolling Russian soldiers. Once I was stopped and sent to an occupied army police station, two hours march in a different direction. There I was given a permit to cross the bridge on the way to the farm. Because of this detour, it took the whole day before I was back at home with my pitcher of milk.

That I could walk unmolested to the farm to get the milk came only after a terrible period of time. As soon as Berlin was in the hands of the Russian troops, they were given "the freedom of the city". This meant total anarchy. The soldiers could steal, torment and rape as they pleased. After a while some discipline was restored and except for some aggravating minor incidents, harassing delays and the early curfew, we were able to start picking up pieces of our daily lives. It was said that women with babies were seldom stopped or molested, so I always took one of my babies with me when it was necessary to go anywhere.

All of Berlin was frightened and tense, so when a woman that I knew in the neighborhood asked if she could take my baby Rainer with her when she had to go someplace, I allowed her to take him that one time. I became so frightened, after spending that anxious after- noon waiting for his return, that I never allowed her to have him again.

The city was in ruins and there was not much in our garden except shrapnel, and it was quite a while before the ration cards for groceries were properly organized and we were able to buy something. There was not enough to live, and too much to die! That was when the black market became a way of life. Absolutely everything was exchanged for groceries! The "hamster" trips started. Train travel was excruciatingly slow but we went anyway, out into the country-side to find if the farmers had any potatoes, eggs — in fact any food we could exchange for the goods we had to offer. Those trips were dangerous as sometimes we were searched, but luckily we were left unharmed; often everything we had would be taken away.

Slowly we settled into a sort of routine: standing for hours in line to buy a loaf of bread, walking for a long time to some distant grocery store that we had heard about and where a certain commodity was to be had, trading via the black market for what we could not get in the store, locking and barricading our doors and windows every evening, doing all the cooking in the short hours when electricity was available and always, always hoping that the Russian soldiers would overlook our home.

We were still digesting the disappointment that it was the Russians and not the American Allied Forces that conquered Berlin. When we had heard the rumble of fighting during the last weeks of the war and knew for certain that the war was lost for Germany, we heard rumors that the Allied Forces were crossing the river Elbe in the West and the Russians the river Oder in the East. We prayed that the Allied Forces were faster than the Russians. Refugees from the eastern parts had told gruesome stories of the behavior of the Russian soldiers.

An aunt and uncle of ours (Lina and Gustav Graap) from Labiau, on the Baltic Sea in East Prussia showed up at our door in December 1945 with their two sons, and with just the things that they could carry. Our house was full before they arrived and now was literally overflowing. They stayed with us a few weeks while trying to find any place in Berlin where the four of them could stay. But when they could not, they took their two young sons and trekked farther west. It was weeks later that they were able to find accommodations in Bremen. But before they left they had many terrible stories to tell of the eastern front and the homestead farm in East Prussia.

They told us that another aunt, Lina, would not leave the farm with her children because she was waiting for my uncle, Friederich (Fritz, mother's brother) to come back from the Eastern front. This aunt waited too long. Her eldest teenage son, Bernhard, barely 15 years old, was taken away by the Russians into the Russian interior. The Russians took all able-bodied young men and boys to work in Russia, and once this boy became sick and was of no further use, he was told to go home. After many months he found his way back to his home, only to die from malnutrition and the vicious beatings he had received by the Russians. Even with non-existent supplies and staples, many home remedies were tried to help this boy, including an old remedy of using spiders' webs as plasters to seal the open sores. After Bernhard died, Aunt Lina and her remaining two young children, Gerda and Walter, were forced from the homestead and found their way to Thuringia, a province south west of Berlin. With the help of the Red Cross her husband, my uncle Fritz, was later re-united with his family only to have his joy at the reunion crushed when he learned about his son's tragic death.

It was long after the war that we learned of the politics involved: Allied Forces could easily have occupied Berlin, but an agreement had been made that would allow Russia to 'get' Berlin. Berlin, as the capital of Germany, was a valuable prize; the closest place to the eastern front, the Allied Forces needed it to keep an eye and ear on the Russians. So the victors exchanged the spoils of war. Thuringia, which the Allies had conquered and the Russians wanted for its raw materials, was traded for half of Berlin, giving the Allies their foothold in East Germany. A fallen Germany was divided into East and West. The once proud city of Berlin was now in Russian East Germany, and with this exchange became a city further divided. Berlin with its West Occupied Sector (American, British and French) became an island within the Russian East zone.

The West Berliners felt sorry for the people in Thuringia as they had experienced the relatively mild occupation by the Americans but now had to suffer under the Russians. Our family gave a huge sigh of relief when we saw the first American soldiers, and we knew for sure that our home was in the West Sector of Berlin.

The famous Potsdam Conference took place just outside Berlin, to the south in the city of Potsdam, which was the seat of the Prussian kings, where the once beautiful castles and palaces graced the landscape and now lay in ruins. It was the summer of 1945, and the fate of a conquered Germany was decided by Churchill, Stalin and Truman, resulting in East and West Germany, East and West Berlin.

With Russian soldiers now leaving West Berlin, we held our breath as we watched them take everything that was not nailed down. We could hardly believe our eyes when they pulled the gooseberry and currant bushes, with half-ripe fruit, out by the roots and carried them away. Relieved to see the Russians leave, we were hoping that the American troops, who were to occupy our sector of the city, would bring some semblance of order to the chaos that reigned after the war. But chaos remained and life consisted of constant changes and turmoil for several years, as we tried to piece our lives together.

The East zone became a state within itself, with new currency introduced for both halves of Germany in 1948. The *Ostmark* for the east and *Dmark* for the west. But first, for a short time it was possible to come and go between the West and East Berlin sectors, although subject to border check points. Then restrictions were put in place and travel into East Germany was no longer allowed. The exception was made for going through the travel corridor that one had to take from West Berlin to the West German Zone, passing directly through the East German Zone. And this was allowed only with special permission. There was one autobahn, and one train connecting West Berlin and West Germany, however there were numerous check points along the route. Few could afford the trip, as gasoline was very expensive and fewer still could afford an auto. There was also an 'air corridor' for aircraft traffic. Suffice to say that travel was limited and difficult. Although the war was over, the city lay in ruins. For now all our thoughts simply turned to the struggle to survive.

Having been laid off from work for a long time already really didn't matter as there was not much to be had and not many staples avail- able anyway. I found a job as a homemaker with an American mother, son and daughter who worked for the U. S. administration of occupied Berlin. I was glad about that, as the folks who worked for the Americans received better ration cards than other German citizens. I was the only one in our family who landed a job with the Americans. My mother was too old for their requirements, so she looked after my two children. My sister Lisa was not allowed to work for the occupation forces because of her Nazi party membership. Between rehabilitation courses, she did find odd jobs here and there, but they were of the most menial kind with very little pay. Christa had left Berlin and Carin was still too young.

My sister Christa was still in Thuringia and we were anxious about her, not sure if she had survived the war. Christa, at the very young age of not quite 16, had started as an apprentice in the research laboratory of the *Spinne* where she was learning to become a chemical lab technician. Due to the constant bombing of Berlin, this department was moved to Bad Schwarza in Thuringia, and Christa went with them. When she finally came home in late 1945, she had been gone for nearly two years. She didn't talk much about her experiences but what she did tell was enough. Nearing the end of the war, the research department was closed, and Christa, now out of work and away from home, was fortunate to find a job at a butter and cheese factory. She became quite hefty and was not caught in the ration-card crunch. At the end of the war, Thuringia was occupied by the American Forces. But as history showed, that did not last long and it was exchanged with the Russians for East Berlin. While Christa had no intention of staying in the Russian Zone, going home to Berlin was a huge problem. There was no transportation. None. So Christa started to walk. There were rivers with no bridges as they had been destroyed. Often it took several days to find a way across. The roads were rough and not to mention, dangerous. The aftermath of the war had left the landscape in ruins and the people in desperate anarchy. As well there were soldiers in various emotional states everywhere! Her nearly 280km walk home took just over three weeks. She never talked much about her experience, and as soon as she came home, she used her time to look for work. Soon she found a job with the occupation forces and became a clerk in one of their offices. With Christa home, we felt fortunate that our family was intact. However I still had not heard any news of Herbert.

The house was crowded, and we were all busy making ends meet. I and my two babies occupied the three small upstairs rooms, while my mother and my three younger sisters occupied the main floor.

Working as a homemaker for an American family didn't allow much time for me to look for a better job, but eventually I was lucky and this luck would help the whole family. Almost around the corner from our house was the administration building of Telefunken. The American army set up their headquarter base here. I was one of the first to apply for a job and managed to get a job as waitress in the officer's mess. For a while I could smuggle an egg or a butter patty to supplement what my mother was able to coax from the garden, or what we could trade on the black market that had crept up everywhere.

Then at the beginning of summer of 1945 my husband Herbert came home. He had been in a prisoner-of-war camp in Bavaria for a short time and then was released to the City of Braunschweig, the last place where his unit was stationed. Again luck held, and after a short time I was able to direct him to a job with the American occupation army in their headquarters at that same Telefunken complex across from our house. That was very fortunate as by now Germans were issued ration cards but they were not of equal value. Laborers and those employed by the American occupation forces received better cards. An added bonus was that we, the German employees, were allowed to eat in the American kitchens! Sometimes we also received American cigarettes. What a Godsend! All this enabled us to use many points of our ration cards and cigarettes for barter. And in exchange for cigarettes we could get almost anything on the black market!

We couldn't speak English but soon learned some essential words to help us try to keep out of trouble. There was much stealing by the civil employees which was semi-tolerated by the Americans. But in the third week of his employment, Herbert had the bad luck to get caught while taking a carton of cigarettes, resulting in his immediate dismissal. It was almost impossible to find a job in the civil sector of the city. However after much fruitless searching, Herbert managed to land a job as an apprentice with a landscaping firm. Berlin was in desperate need of clean up, rubble removal and landscaping. An apprenticeship was usually a three year term but since Herbert had the *Abitur* (equivalent to our grade 13), he was only required to sign a contract for a two year term.

For a short while life became more or less routine. Mother looked after Monika and Rainer while we worked. To augment my financial contribution I also paid her with leftovers I managed to bring home from the mess hall: bits of sugar, jam, even old coffee grounds which were re-used by us. There was also raw bread dough and bacon drippings, all impossible to obtain in any regular way. It was risky to find leftovers to take home. Some Americans turned a blind eye, but other soldiers were not so gracious and simply dumped everything into the trash and smiled back at the hungry German waitresses. Going home at the end of a shift was always an anxious time, you could lose your job over a cube of sugar.

Beside my work at the mess hall, I took in laundry for the American soldiers. That way the soap, which they supplied, made its way to our home. Soap was another commodity that could not be had any other way. By way of payment an America soldier once gave me a khaki army blanket and that was truly a gift from heaven! Our ration cards for textiles was so meager that there was never enough points to buy things for the ever-growing children. We had a distant relative who was a tailor and in exchange for stuff from the mess hall, he made winter coats for Monika and Rainer from that blanket.

During all these months Herbert was withdrawn and restless. I put it down to the time in the war, the terrible and unstable job situation, and his possible resentment of having to rely on my income and the tidbits I brought home. His pay as a landscape apprentice was not enough even to buy bread on the black market. Then a letter from Braunschweig fell into my hands and all became clear. The letter was written by a married woman who asked Herbert if he could arrange to take the son that he had with her. Her long-absent husband was to arrive shortly from a prisoner-of-war camp. This son, also named Herbert, was born at the same time as our second child, Rainer, give or take a few days! Totally shocked and devastated, I did not know what to do, I couldn't work, I couldn't think. Simply occupied with day-to-day survival and not mature or wise enough to deal with this situation, I went to my father-in-law for advice. He advised me to wait a bit and let the dust settle before making any decision. But before a decision could be made, the baby Herbert died in Braunschweig. A huge rift that could not be healed had opened between my husband and me. I sued for divorce and Herbert moved back with his parents.

Not long after Herbert left, young Erika, Herbert's sister came to visit me. She asked me to sign a typewritten declaration that she brought with her. It stated that all the furniture in my home was rented from my parents-in-law, Wilhelm and Else Stimming. But in fact some of the furniture was a wedding gift from Helene Stimming, Herbert's grandmother, who had given me the diamond ring at our first meeting. The explanation that Erika gave me was that the American forces were known to requisition furniture for their quarters and with this signed declaration they could not. It would show the furniture to be on loan from people within the Russian sector of Berlin, where Herbert's family now lived. The whole thing was complete non- sense but it shows my state of mind as I signed the paper believing her story.

A few weeks later I came home from work to find my mother in tears and my small upstairs apartment completely empty. Not a baby bed left, even the wall covers of the electric sockets had been removed! My mother said that two men arrived with a truck and with the piece of paper that I had signed. They took everything. Exactly whose idea this was I never found out.

After the shock of that Braunschweig letter, everything in my life began spinning quickly. When I no longer worked as a waitress in the mess, I was fortunate enough to be hired as a translator in the pack- ing and crating division of the American occupation forces. It was not necessary to be fluent in English what was required was to type the manifests in English. It was better pay, and that made up for the loss of food stuff that I had managed to bring home from the mess. So much had happened in the short time of a few weeks. And then I found out that I was pregnant again. With my emotions and life in turmoil, I was helped by a girlfriend, who was also a doctor.

Herbert's parents, who took my side in our marital conflict, refused to subsidize him while he was an apprentice at the landscape firm. This was an especially hard time for Herbert, and he was forced to break his apprentice contract which was not easily done. So he told his employer that his parents were so devastated about the upcoming divorce that they took their lives by gas poisoning, leaving him with no means to live without their financial help. He was relieved of the contract. I came upon this outrageous lie quite by accident much later. A driver at the packing and crating department, who had previously worked for the same landscaping firm, noted my name, and with one breath he asked if I was related to Herbert Stimming, and how sorry he was for the loss of my parents-in-law!

It was many months of unemployment before Herbert eventually landed a job as driver for a milk-delivery van. It might have been with is aunt Kaethe, who managed the Stimming dairy business with her husband, but I never asked.

In due time the divorce became final, and in all this time I never lost contact with my parents-in-law. They came to visit Monika and Rainer, and the children even stayed with them at different times. My sister-in-law, Erika, was also a frequent visitor in my home, which was still at my mother's house. For the children the divorce changed little in their young lives. Furniture means nothing to children and we were able to spread what little furniture was left with my mother downstairs, and re-arrange it to make do. Herbert had been absent for most of our marriage due to the turbulent times that Germany was in, and the hardships of divorce merely added to the hardships of the war. That Herbert showed little interest in the children was just another fact.

Then began the year 1946 which was to bring the hardest winter in a long, long time. There were no heating materials to be had, when one avenue opened and gave us a chance to get some wood. The Grunewald, the large forest laying between the outskirts of West Berlin and the river Havel, was severely damaged by the bombing. The broken- down trees had been long removed and now only the stumps and huge roots were left. The forest department decided to make those stumps and roots available to the public for the princely sum of 25 Deutsche Mark (DM) per stump or root. That fulfilled a three-fold purpose: the department got the area cleaned, made a bit of sorely- needed money, and the public got the even more urgently required heating material.

I worked a double shift and a colleague worked another day for me so that I could have one day off. My sister Lisa and I borrowed a hand wagon from a neighbor and with pick and shovel in hand, we began walking before dawn to Grunewald. We paid our 25 DM and started digging. It took an entire day just to free one root. They were huge and hard as iron, as the trees were mostly oak and maple. It was nightfall before we made it home with our load. Then the hard task began. We had to cut and saw the root into manageable pieces that would fit into our stove. Every day after work, my sister and I were sawing and hacking away at the root.

We went to Grunewald once a week for five weeks and repeated this process. Then we were too exhausted to do any more or even to care. But our efforts paid off. We had some means to keep warm this coming winter. But it proved to be not enough. Although I dressed my children warmly for the nights, Rainer, who tossed and turned a lot in his sleep froze a spot on his cheek which for many years thereafter showed itself as a white spot on his cheek as soon as the cold weather came. A few times, through the Care organization, we were able to acquire some pieces of coal. These precious pieces were tightly wrapped in newspaper and put on the burning wood. This was done to maximize the burning time with the hope of just a little more heat for a little longer.

But even in those terrible days, little blessings occurred. My mother, sisters and I looked forward to our evenings when the children were safely asleep. During those precious moments together sitting around our dining room table, we felt closer than we would for much of the rest of our lives. The electricity was out and by the light of an old- fashioned oil lamp, as we did our endless mending of socks and precious clothing, we would take turns reading aloud from a book. That was a real treat as we were all hungry for food to feed the mind.

The city was just slowly beginning to operate. Movie theaters, museums and other luxury entertainment centers were not operating, and even if there was one, they would be difficult and awkward for us to reach. However a library was open nearby and we were some of its best customers. This reading and working brought us closer to each other, and these hours of togetherness were what I missed most in the first years when I finally left my birth home.

After the divorce from Herbert, and while I worked as translator with the crating and shipping department of the American army, my life began to glue back together. The routine of work, children and the many chores at home were soothing. A comradeship began to develop among the German workers at the American army base. That department packed and crated the luggage of the officers of the American forces who were going back home to the United States. There were four men who did the packing and one secretary who typed the lists of contents for each crate. That secretary was me and Josef Koenigsberger was one of the craters. We became friends.

FOUR

1946 - 1954

Rebuilding with Josef

Directly after World War II, when Germany was in a broken turmoil and my personal life lay in ruins, the fact that my children, my mother, sisters and I had all survived the war, and we were all still together, was a blessing. That the American base was directly across from our home was another. My daily struggles eventually led me to the job of translator/secretary at the American forces packing and crating department. The rubble that was Berlin, the emptiness, sorrow and confusion, and broken lives had everyone thankful for whatever they had and for some of us, looking for some glimmers of light. I found real delight and an entertaining diversion from the daily toil, and that came by way of my co-workers.

Josef Koenigsberger was one of the fellows who boxed and hammered together the large wooden crates, and I was the secretary who wrote up the manifests listing the contents of these big boxes. Anyone who remembers Josef will tell you of his humor but also of his quick temper. His eagerness to get a job done would often result in shortcuts, and the innovations that he created were often humorous in themselves. It was his energy that was punctuated with a light-heartedness that attracted me and the attraction was mutual. The war years left everyone in a hurry to get on with life and this attraction quickly developed into a courtship that led to marriage, a marriage that lasted for 44 years. Of course there was the turmoil that every marriage has, but we were blessed with his fun-loving ways. However, as I reflect back, it was his strong sense of responsibility that I am truly grateful for.

Every life has its beginning with a family history, childhood and exciting youth, but it is the adolescent years that shape us. My generation, an entire mass of people, has been shaped by and felt the effect of growing to maturity during the war years. Individually and collectively the war years left their mark on all of Europe, the allied countries, Russia and the Middle East. Every person, without exception has his story.

There is little known of Josef's family history, but I can tell you that Josef's father, Johann Koenigsberger had a good friend, Arthur Nehls. Although Johann is listed as a tailor by profession on his marriage certificate, these two men worked, right after the First World War, in the *Hilfspolizei,* a sub-division of the regular police. While stationed in Upper Silesia, in what is now Poland, these two friends met and married two sisters, Martha Wilde and Elli Wilde.

Johann married Martha and they became Josef's parents, while Arthur married Elli and several years later they had a daughter, Lydia. The two sisters had an aunt who had moved to Berlin, and when Elli married Arthur, Elli insisted on moving to Berlin too, while Johann and Martha remained for a while longer in Upper Silesia. This aunt in Berlin, Paula Gajowsky, was a very interesting lady. Many years later, after Josef and I were married, we would often visit with her. Paula, who never married, was always a very independent and hard-working woman. She became quite well-to-do in the thriving black market that developed after the second world war, as she used the divided Germany to her advantage. In East Germany there was a ready market for all sorts of medicines that were unavailable. She would buy over the counter medicine in West Berlin and sell them for a substantially high profit in the East, though the now famous Berlin Wall put an end to that. But I'm getting ahead of myself.

Josef was born on February 27, 1923 in Koenigshutte, in Upper Silesia. At the time of his birth, Koenigshutte was part of Germany, but shortly afterwards it was given to Poland as part of the World War I peace treaty. There is no documentation available for Upper Silesia and there was no communication between West Germany and Poland after World War II, so Josef did not have a birth certificate. In later years when he needed a certificate, he was simply issued a paper from Hamburg, West Germany, stating that there was no documentation from Poland available!

Josef's father, Johann, was born in Neumarkt, Bavaria and his mother Martha, was born in Koenigshuttte, Upper Silesia, where they met and married. With every war there is upheaval and migration of people. The time right after the First World War, when Josef was born, was no exception.

They decided to leave as Upper Silesia was to become annexed to Poland. However Martha wanted to move to Berlin where her aunt and sister were, but Johann wanted to return to his birthplace in Bavaria, which is one of the two southernmost states in Germany.

Martha and Johann's marriage broke down. There may have been several contributing factors, but the exact reason is not known to me. Martha, Oma-Martha to my children, once said that she only wanted a child, and as she was a Catholic it would have been a great sin to have a child out of wedlock. I think this was a way of putting an end to the conversation and I never pursued the topic further. When I look at the records I have today, Martha was born to her parents three days before they married. I suspect that her mother had felt some stigma about being unmarried, pregnant and Catholic, and maybe there had been some conversation on this during Martha's childhood. In any case, Martha left her husband Johann, and took her tiny six-month-old baby Josef to Berlin.

The four-story walk-up apartment house where her sister, Elli, with husband Arthur, had a small flat, had many apartments, and it was also where ' Tante' Paula lived. Martha and baby Josef went to live with Paula. It took some time, but later Martha managed to get her own small apartment in that same building in the middle of downtown Berlin. Josef grew up and lived his entire childhood, until the war, in that same apartment house, as did this small extended family: Great- aunt Paula, Uncle Arthur, Aunt Elli and later their daughter Lydia.

Johann, after returning to Neumarkt remarried and had four more children. But sadly Josef's mother never revealed any information about Josef's father to him. Josef grew up as an only child with just his mother and neighbors to nurture him as he matured through those turbulent years that was Germany, in the middle of downtown Berlin. Later, as Josef was determined to find out more about his family, when he and I were married we traveled on a belated honey- moon of sorts, and in 1948 went to search out his long-lost relatives.

We met Johann's second wife and some of Josef's step-siblings, who were also grown up by then. But sadly by that time Johann, Josef's father, had already died. His mother had never told him anything about his father's side of the family, and she did not allow Josef to have any contact with his father while he was growing up. Although she knew, she did not even tell Josef about his father's death.

In Neumarkt we were able to meet Josef's grandfather who was retired and blind. Josef's grandfather now lived with Georg, his other son, and it was Georg's family who cared for the aging blind patriarch.

In his younger years and before this grandfather had become blind and retired, he had a mobile shop. He loaded all kinds of house- hold goods, baskets, pails, cooking pots and pans, cutlery and dishes on a horse-drawn wagon, and made his rounds to the villages and outlying farmhouses. He would take orders on one trip and deliver the goods on the next. It was not unusual at that time, during the early 1900's, to do business with horse and wagon, wandering from house-to-house, village-to-village and the outlying farms and homesteads to service people who had no other means of shopping. This business was prosperous and allowed the Koenigsberger's to buy several houses in Newmarkt. In those days Newmarkt was about the size of a small town with more than a couple thousand people living there. So it had made sense for Johann, Josef's father, to wish to return after the upheaval of the First World War and Poland's annexation. Life for Josef would have been very different if he had grown up in Newmarkt rather than in the downtown metropolis of Berlin with a single mother!

During this trip in 1948 we also had an opportunity to meet two of Josef's many half-siblings. We met Rupert and Gilda while we were in Hausen, von de Rhoen, and we stayed in contact with the family for several years until once again communication became difficult. It wasn't until 1980 that my youngest sister, Carin, and her husband were able to see them one more time while they were travelling through Bavaria. Travel was still difficult, and it was good news that they were able to locate the family again and find them all well and living. I wrote to the family after that and even sent some photos of Josef and our family, but sadly I never received an answer.

Josef's story begins in late summer of 1923, when Martha and her baby Josef settled with her aunt, Paula, in her downtown Berlin apartment. At that time Paula earned her living managing all of the restrooms at the Haus Vaterland Hotel. Berlin was famous for its lively entertainment centers, and this hotel was one of the most famous hotels in Berlin. It was directly across the street from their apartment building, in what is known as Potsdammer Platz. With Paula's assistance, Martha got a job as seamstress, repairing linens and costumes for Haus Vaterland.

I have no idea who looked after the baby Josef while Martha worked sewing across the street, but I was told that there were many times when he was simply left in his crib for hours on end. Maybe Martha and her aunt worked shifts or maybe Martha's sister, Elli, helped to look after him, when she could. It seems that his early childhood years revolved around that small extended family and the busy work schedules of these adults as they all had flats in that apartment house. By the time that Josef was five years old, he was no longer the only child. His aunt Elli and uncle Arthur were blessed with a baby daughter, Lydia. Even though she was five years younger than Josef, these cousins grew up together and were close friends, a friendship that continued long into adulthood even through the distance of relocation overseas. In 1947, just before I married Josef, Lydia married an American soldier who was stationed in Berlin and they moved to Wilmington, Delaware in the United States. Lydia and my children continue to visit to this day.

Life for Martha consisted of work and her son. She was content to have her sister and her family as close as the apartment next door. Then Martha befriended a gentleman who made all sorts of buttons. Martha never re-married and there was no mention of a boyfriend, but this gentleman became a close family friend. He was well off and had a cottage on one of the many lakes around Berlin, and when Josef was a young child she took him there quite often. Josef's childhood was free as he was often left to entertain himself. He was allowed to use the little rowboat at the lake, and had many little adventures. Once, as a very young boy, he lost the oars. Luckily he was not far from shore and pulled himself back by the reeds to the dock and safety. When the reality of the danger became apparent, it was a long time before he was permitted to take the boat out again.

But his lifelong love of boats and water took root. All during his adult life he was never long without a boat of his own. Right up until he died in January 1990 he always had a boat, be it a canoe, row-boat, motor boat, cruiser or sailboat. In lean years he would salvage a small boat and, after extensive and labor-intensive repairs, launch it at the nearest lake or river at every free moment he had. In the best of years, just before his retirement, he managed to acquire the most beautiful sailboat which was the envy of many a yachtsman.

Josef's life growing up in the center of Berlin (aside from these few excursions to that lakeside cottage) was concrete, pavement and brick apartment buildings with all the hustle and noise of downtown life. Martha was not well off but as a single mother with Josef her only child, she was as over-indulgent as she could be. He was allowed to eat donuts for breakfast and have a considerable amount of freedom. Roaming from one apartment to another visiting his great-aunt and also to Lydia's home, he had the good fortune to have the attention of many "mothers". Although over-indulgent in many ways, Martha was also a concerned mother. A bicycle in that downtown environment was out of the question. But after much pleading and coaxing she eventually relented and allowed his great-aunt Paula to finally give him one. The traffic, crowded streets and Josef's quick and boisterous manner caused many worries for the mild and gentle Martha.

By this time, Martha had her own apartment. I don't know how many rooms that apartment had but there must have been enough, because Martha often rented a room to the entertainers who worked at the theater in the nearby Haus Vaterland. Because these entertainers needed to rehearse, Martha managed to put a piano in that room for them. Josef, curious as he was, picked up various musical skills and developed a sense of humor and entertainment. These entertainers had time and enthusiasm for young Josef and he lapped up the attention, soon learning to play tunes on the piano and he even learned the accordion. It is regrettable that he never had a chance to take real training and learn to read music, but his keen sense of music and his diligence paid off as he was able to entertain at many a house party for the rest of his life. In later years he played the harmonica and even acquired a mandolin, which he played quite well. But his favorite instrument was always the accordion.

Aside from Josef's mother, his friends and Lydia's family, it was his great-aunt Paula who played a major role in his young life. She was the one who finally got him his bicycle, over his mother's object-ions, but she also looked out for him in many other ways as well. It was she who took him on his first visit to Haus Vaterland.

Haus Vaterland was a well known and prestigious establishment. It was an entertainment center *extraordinaire*! It boasted numerous restaurants, each one with a different ambiance. There were Italian

Bistros, Vienna pastry *Stuben*, French sidewalk cafes, Moroccan coffee houses, Munich beer cellars and so on. The place was huge! Each restaurant was decorated according to its theme with waiters and waitresses dressed in the theme's local costumes and serving the appropriate foods. Each restaurant boasted a live band that entertained its customers with local songs and music to compliment the theme. During the 1920's and 1930's Berlin was renowned for its lively entertainment and clubs, with Haus Vaterland often receiving top revues. There was constant work for Martha repairing the linens and a never-ending parade of costumes that required alterations. These entertainers and some of the musicians rented a room from Martha during their engagements, were the ones who inspired Josef to play music. But it was his great-aunt Paula who introduced Josef to real theater culture, and the impression of that first visit left him with memories of wonderment, excitement and awe.

Josef was about five or six years old when his great-aunt first took him on his first visit. And Josef, who was often left to amuse himself, had vivid and lasting memories of the special attention Tante Paula showered on him. Before taking him to Haus Vaterland she took him to a large department store, Wertheim, on the other side of Potsdammer Platz. It should be noted that the whole Potsdammer Platz went up in smoke and ruin during the Second World War. What the bombs didn't destroy, the street fighting towards the end of the war finished and the famous Haus Vaterland was nothing but rubble. Later this empty area became no-man's land between the wall and the two sides of Berlin.

Great-aunt Paula took Josef to Wertheim, a store akin to Harrods in London, and bought him new clothes as she did not like the well-worn clothes he was wearing. She bought him the entire outfit and accessories, underwear, socks, suit and shoes. Then she took him in his finery to the fabled Haus Vaterland. This visit, first to the department store and then to the entertainment center was Josef's fondest childhood memory. It impressed him to no end and he behaved as the little gentleman that he was.

Josef, unaccustomed to formal dinners as his meal times were mostly on the run, had a memory that he was not so fond of, when he embarrassed his great-aunt and her guests at the dinner table. The table was set with a beautiful lace-edged tablecloth, the great-aunt's best china, silver and numerous dishes with carefully prepared food. Josef for some reason became fidgety and decided to leave the table. As he got up, he did not notice that the lace edge of the tablecloth had caught on the button of his shorts. He dragged the tablecloth with everything on it and was almost at the door before he noticed the disaster. Blushing hotly to the roots of his hair and in his haste to disentangle himself, he ripped the button off and fled. He never told me what happened to him afterward. If he was punished or reprimanded it was never mentioned but the embarrassment of the moment stayed in his mind, and after hearing this story I understood why he never fully enjoyed formal meals. Even though he laughed when he told the story, the picture of the beautiful and carefully prepared dinner on the floor was enough to make me cringe.

Josef's school friend Georg, whom Josef nicknamed "Pippin", was to become a long-standing friend well into adulthood. In fact the whole of Georg's family became an extended family for Josef. As teenagers, these two best friends acquired a row-boat as Pippin loved the outdoors, especially the water, as much as Josef. They stored it just south-east of Berlin, on Lake Mueggelsee, one of the many around Berlin. Every Saturday, as soon as school was out, they would pedal their bicycles for over an hour to the boathouse and the boat. They would load it with their tent and other gear, and set out to explore the many beautiful waterways around Berlin. They continued these outings through their apprenticeship and even later when they began to work. Eventually they managed to get a small motor for that boat and their excursions took on a new dimension as they put-putted to their various destinations with a little greater speed. Some- times they met up with other young people and camped in groups. In those days apprenticeship began right after high school, at about fourteen years, and by sixteen one was fully launched into the adult working world. Still teenagers and young at heart, their boating excursions provided the fun, freedom and excitement to recharge for the hard work of daily life.

But the war quickly put an end to these heavenly excursions. As soon as the Second World War began gasoline was rationed with nothing allowed for pleasure trips. If that wasn't enough to dampen the young men's spirits, during one of the first air raids by the Allied forces on Berlin, the boathouse where they stored their boat was struck. All was destroyed, the little boat as well as the boathouse were nothing but rubble.

Living in that same apartment house Josef had another friend named Erich Jescheke. Erich had a motorcycle. Together they would go for tours through the city or outskirts of Berlin. Often Erich allowed Josef to take the motorbike on his own but the war put an end to these trips too. Erich, who was much older than Josef, was a father-figure to him and much later at our wedding in 1948 Erich was our best man.

I tried so hard to forget all that happened during the war, and it is hard for me to write about it, but what happened to Josef is even more difficult to write. I met Josef after the war and what I can tell about Josef is only what he told me. At first, during our courtship and marriage he didn't talk about his experiences. It was much later and even then, it was only on a few occasions, that he would talk about those times.

When the war started in 1939 he was sixteen years old and still in apprenticeship with a master carpenter. The first indication for him that war meant hardship was when gas was rationed and no petrol was allowed for pleasure. With his little outboard motor, and the motorcycle he borrowed stored in the basement of the apartment house, it was frustrating for the young teen not to be able to go on excursions; but when a bomb hit and destroyed the boat and boat- house, the reality of war began to sink in.

The apartment house which was home to Josef was in the very center of Berlin. And when Josef and I married there was little that he could show me of his childhood home or neighborhood. All was destroyed by the bombs during the war. The entire area was a huge rubble heap. The Haus Vaterland, Wertheim (the huge shopping center) and the famous big clock that was known as a meeting place for young couples — everything everywhere was rubble. One night early in the war, one night everything that Josef and his mother owned was destroyed. Twice more his mother was bombed out losing all her painstakingly assembled belongings. It was a blessing that no one in that small family lost their life.

But the bombing and destruction of Josef's home happened when he was already in the Air Force. He had volunteered for the Luftwaffe to avoid being drafted to the infantry. Imagine, twice he came home to visit his mother only to find ruins, but luckily, after frantically searching and questioning, both times he was able to find her again.

Noting that Josef was a clever man, the Luftwaffe trained him as one of the team that assembled the V2 rockets. (V2 means *Vergel- tungswaffe,* or retribution weapon). Germany hoped that the V2, which is the unmanned rocket that was fired at England's cities, would be a major success for Germany. The V2 was developed and tested in Peenemuende but assembled in Wolfsburg, in deepest secrecy. There were underground warehouses and assembly production areas. For security reasons the soldiers working on the V2 had to wear civilian clothes. They carried special permits allowing them to pass as they were inevitably stopped by military police. And they were stopped regularly as these soldiers, Josef among them, were young, healthy and of the right military age and could, in their civilian clothes, be considered deserters and as such could be hauled before a military tribunal. But because Josef and the soldiers were not informed and kept ignorant, all this didn't become clear to him until much later. The assembly of the V2 was carried out in bits and pieces and no one really knew what they were working on.

Josef's soldier's book shows that there were many trips made in civilian clothes. Often these trips were for military reasons, and secret errands, and his book shows these trips listed for a variety of illnesses and personal reasons. As a soldier you followed orders and as a soldier, who was allocated to civilian clothes, he found that he had orders to run errands. He talked very little about these times, but I'm sure the stress and adventures shaped his mannerisms that I knew to be quick yet attentive, friendly but always alone, independent and cautious.

At first they lived in barracks but soon these men were allowed to look for private quarters. Josef and his friend, Karl-Heinz Gebhardt, were billeted together. The landlord had a young daughter, and soon Josef and this girl were passionately in love. Josef took many risks to be with this girl, even using a forged pass as he took her to Berlin for a night on the town. They became engaged. But luckily for me, she did not wait for Josef. When Josef was reported missing-in-action at the end of the war, she married and in short order had four children.

All the time when Josef was working on the V2, his aim was to become a pilot. He volunteered for any course that was available. He developed a skill with all things mechanical and had a love for any kind of motor. But he was never able to realize his dream of becoming a pilot as one of his eyes was not up to par and he had difficulty focusing.

So, Josef was relatively safe during most of the war, at least until near the end. However his mother in Berlin had to endure much hardship. Living in the center of Berlin she first experienced the many allied bomb attacks that leveled the city, and then later the chaos from the invading Russians. Survival was paramount and as I think back, although my family had very tough times, we were living away from the center of Berlin, with the possibility of a garden, but Martha suffered greatly in the struggle to survive in the rubble of concrete and brick. She had to manage on the meager ration cards, scrounging for necessities during the most difficult times when there was nothing but destruction everywhere.

Towards the end of the war all available men were put into the infantry. Josef had to leave the Air Force to be assigned to an infantry regiment. Still, he was not involved in too much fighting, not until the very end of the war. He was in the trenches in the south-east of France when those trenches were overrun by American forces and he was taken prisoner.

Along with tens of thousands of prisoners-of-war he was taken to the infamous Camp #401 near Marseille. It was a vast plateau, empty of trees or structures. They slept in the dirt, in holes that they man- aged to dig for themselves. There were no blankets. There were no latrines. There was no food or water for days. A great number of prisoners died there. The first to die were the intellectuals, doctors, scientists, professors, and folks from the wealthy sector of society. They could not adapt to the harsh treatment and living environment. Much is written of the history of these prisoner-of-war camps and how the harsh conditions and lack of food contributed to greatly reducing the numbers of German prisoners.

Finally along with some supplies that were eventually brought there, the men were organized to bring some order out of the chaos. White bread and cream of wheat was the first food the prisoners had in many, many days. These first meals brought on diarrhea because of the effects of starvation and lack of water. After the initial distribution of food and in the first few days that followed, the men were organized into groups to make shelters as tents were erected. And the dead had to be buried.

Then latrines were dug, and finally there seemed to be some sort of haphazard direction. Finally, when the thousands of men were organized, those with some skills were chosen to work in the kitchens, makeshift hospitals and the various workshops.

Although there were thousands of men, each was alone in their plight. Many years later and far away from Germany, Josef met another who had been in that same camp. I remember their initial recognition when a brief conversation indicated that they had both been among these prisoners, and although they remained friends for the rest of their lives, neither Josef nor Alfons ever talked about their experience again.

Josef quickly learned to volunteer for any work that came up, and felt himself to be extremely lucky when he was selected to work in a shoe repair shop. Here all sorts of leather goods were repaired; boots, shoes, belts, handles for knapsacks and even tent latches. But he had never done such work before and was soon found out. This turned into a stroke of incredible luck as he was now moved to help in the kitchen tent. Here his weight was to reach its highest point in all his life! But eventually he was posted to a machine shop where his skills and knowledge of motors came to good use.

One prisoner, who was released early for some reason, went to visit Josef's mother in Berlin. Upon telling her how her son looked and worked as a prisoner-of-war, she wrote to him begging him to stay there as long as possible. Berlin was in total destruction, there was no living space for him and there was no food whatsoever. She could barely keep herself alive.

Josef, who was born in Königshütte, which was given to Poland after the First World War, was registered as a Polish national, enabling his release when the Americans released all the prisoners who were not German first. Most German soldiers upon being captured destroyed their soldiers' books, but Josef had a premonition and kept his. As he did not wish to be shipped to Poland, he had to convince the American officers that he was German. He explained that he was taken out of Königshütte as a baby and lived all his life as a German in Berlin. The American officers, who tried to speak Polish to him, made no sense to him as Josef had never spoke anything but German. Eventually he managed to convince them that he should be released as a German to Berlin. But that was another problem. Berlin was now in the Russian occupied zone and no one was released to Berlin. Somehow with his persuasiveness he managed to be released to Frankfurt/Main, and his nearly two-year stay at the American prisoner-of-war camp was over.

At Frankfurt/Main he found work on a small farm where he stayed for about a year. Here he was able to apply for the very necessary ration cards, and at the end of that year he set out to find his way back to Berlin, a difficult journey of which he rarely spoke. Germany was now divided into East and West. He had to travel through Russian East Germany to get to Berlin, a city which itself was further divided into the occupied sectors. Once in Berlin, he was shocked by the dismal conditions. He became bitter and disillusioned. It was sheer luck that his mother, who had been bombed out in the Russian Sector, had found a place to live in the American Sector.

After many futile attempts to find work, Josef found himself in the huge unemployment line at the American Army base. Almost overlooked and afraid of not landing a job, he was extremely nervous when nearly all the men had been selected and he was one of the men left still waiting. There were only two crating positions still available and an inner will within Josef demanded to be heard. In a bold and anxious voice he stated that his pre-war apprenticeship was for a carpenter's trade and that it should be taken into consideration. "Doesn't hammering the crates shut require a carpenter's skill?" He got the job. This army base was located across the road from my home. And this was the base where I was working as a translator-secretary writing the manifests of those very crates he was to nail together.

Although the war was over, these were difficult times. Berlin was still very much in ruins. These were also the times that heralded the beginning of the cold war era. It was the time when the Russians blockaded every road and train into West Berlin, and West Berliners were completely barred from entry into East Berlin. The Russians had isolated West Berlin from the rest of the world! That meant that no consumer goods whatsoever could reach the West Berlin Sector. Along with the many other shortcomings electricity was also rationed; only very brief periods of electricity were made available for the citizens as there was not enough coal to operate the huge power generators.

Berlin was choking. For us Berliners, who had survived the war years and the relentless bombing, the hunger and lack of any consumer goods, or even jobs to buy anything … we found ourselves desperate again after such a brief time of trying to get some sort of routine to our existence. Although we West Berliners were more than a little concerned that we might fall back into Russian hands, we were sure that the western world would not allow it. And when Lucias Clay, an American general, had the idea to bring all the goods necessary for the survival of West Berlin into Berlin via airplanes, we were heartily grateful, for our immediate concern was not the political implications, but rather concern for the necessities of life!

The *Luft* corridor was one access to West Berlin that the Russians could not control. Thus, the now famous, "Air Lift for Berlin" began. The survival of West Berlin was an essential political necessity for the rest of the western world. So, everything from powdered milk to raw material for the industries was shipped in by air. The effort was an enormous undertaking and one that had never been done before. The whole operation was called the *Luftbruecke* (Air Bridge), and was a commitment made by the Americans, who organized the dedicated pilots from Britain, Canada and France that was to last for several months.

The Templehof Air Field, the air-port in the middle of West Berlin was to handle the landing of one plane a minute. Several pilots lost their lives in the cramped take off and landings. Today a monument at the entrance of the Templehof Air Field pays homage to the many pilots, and in Zhelendorf, a main street is named after Lucias Clay as the people of West Berlin shall always remember the efforts to keep West Berlin alive. Never before, or since, did we in the Western Zone of Berlin feel as much like an island in the Russian Zone than at that time. We never forgot the prompt and efficient help from the west.

After several months of this extraordinary effort by the western allies, the Russians gave in and the roads to West Berlin were re- opened. However the Russians were not going to make travel easy; many restrictions were implemented and civilian travels severely limited.

Josef and I had an intense relationship. We worked together and in the evenings when my mother was able to look after my children, Monika and Rainer, Joe and I dated. By this time some movie theaters were open and dance halls once again were filled to capacity as every young person tried to forget the war and the times we found ourselves in.

Joe and I even went to a live theater once, but he was so bored that we never went again. With all the shortcomings of life in Berlin, we were never short of money although what we could buy was another challenge. We could supplement our already superior German ration cards and our good wages earned while working for the Americans. And to top it off we could sell our American cigarettes that we received as tips from the Americans for whom we packed! We worked and we lightened up the desperate years we had survived, and although things were never easy, we had fun and we courted. The ups and downs, the war years, the hard work took its toll on my health, and somehow I didn't realize I was pregnant again until well into my sixth month.

In February 1948, Joe and I were married, and Irene arrived shortly thereafter on May 19. Joe, an only child, now found himself with a large ready-made family and all the responsibilities that came with it. He moved into my family home, now occupied by me and my two children, but also my mother and three sisters, Lisa, Christa and Carin. So, at the ripe age of 25, Josef instantly became the man of the house, with five women, two children and a baby. My mother, the matriarch of the family, continued to rule and Josef accepted his responsibilities but not without difficulty; I'm sure he longed for his freedom as a bachelor.

Occasionally Josef would go off with his friends to relieve some of the stress of living in such close quarters with so many women and children. A rare motorcycle trip into the Russian zone almost ended in disaster. Alcoholic beverages were dirt cheap in the Russian Zone, almost making you think that this was a way for the Russians to appease the unhappy people. Josef and his friend's adventure led from bar to bar as they traveled through the zone until well past midnight. Then while trying to navigate home in the dark, on the broken roads, they encountered an unmarked construction area. At full speed they fell approximately seven feet down into a huge pit. Drunk, disoriented, lucky to have only bruises, and in a hurry to get out of the Russian zone, they hoisted themselves and their motor- cycle up the steep sides of this enormous hole. It took quite a while but eventually in the early hours of the morning they managed to arrive home.

Josef was often late coming home from his excursions, and I, newly married and upset, took his house key. Though I fell asleep alone, he would be there beside me in the morning. How he got back into the house was, for a long time, a puzzle. Then one day while trying to enter by his usual route, via a ladder against the house leading to the opening for the chimney-sweep trap door, a policeman happened to see him on the roof. Thinking that Josef was a burglar, he beckoned Josef to come down and show identification. Josef, who had none with him, tried to explain that he lived here and pleaded, "please, don't be so loud and wake my wife". So the police told him to go ahead, enter the house via the roof and come out immediately, this time via the door, with the identification. Naturally this time I woke up. Taking his key away had been totally useless. Frustrations and responsibilities caused many stormy arguments; in later years our memories of these times were a great source of entertainment and laughter.

Josef did not always go off by himself with his buddies and some- times when another member of my family was free to look after my children, I went on the town with him. Once when we both wanted to go to a movie, my cousin joined us. As Josef thought the movie theater was too far to walk, he decided that the three of us should ride on the motorcycle. It was mid winter and the roads were icy … very icy by the time the movie was over. The three of us with all our feet dragging on the ground to steady the bike, were concentrating so intensely to keep it upright, that we didn't even notice the police car following us. When we finally arrived at our gate the police stopped us and said that if we would have fallen we would have all been charged. They stated that they were so impressed with Josef's driving skills, that they let us go with just a warning. None of this seemed to bother us, we were young and full of adventure, the war was over and danger was not a consideration.

Then came the winter of 1949 and there was still very little heat- ing fuel available. We had some wood and a little coal but needed more coal to keep the fires in our little heaters going, and this was a very cold winter. As luck would have it, my best friend from school, Gertrude Hammermeister, had become mayor of Potsdam. But unfortunately Potsdam, although just south of Zehlendorf, where we lived, was in the East (Russian) Zone. She had access and connections to an area where coal was available. We were apt to meet with less hassle at the checkpoints crossing into the Eastern Zone if we went by bicycle rather than by motorcycle, so as often as we could, Josef and I peddled our bicycles to Potsdam and filled our backpacks with coal. It was a round trip of eight hours from the time we left our house and returned with our precious bundles. I still have a scar in the middle of my back as a memento of these trips. As I was pedaling the coal dust would work its way through the backpack, through my clothes and then rub my skin raw beneath my bra. A huge and painful sore developed. My regular doctor took one look and said it was way too deep and beyond his expertise to treat, so he sent me to a military doctor who was familiar with all types of obnoxious war wounds.

Often serious issues turned humorous. With winter here Josef needed a coat, a decent looking coat, as he was always looking for work. An uncle was a tailor and as consumer goods were still scarce, we had to improvise. We had an army blanket that the kids slept on. This could be replaced with an old one that we repaired and the blanket was then tailored into a beautiful fitting coat for Josef. The only problem was that every time it rained or when it snowed the coat became damp and smelled, you guessed it like a baby's wet diaper.

With clothing so difficult to get, I was constantly unraveling our knitted things and re-knitting as the children grew. Afghans became little sweaters. Sweaters became dresses. The girls, Monika and Irene, had beautiful skirts that I knitted. They were patterned with different colored circles and when the children grew, I just added another circle.

Finally in 1950 the *Spinnstoffabrik* re-opened production again. It had taken five years to remedy the war destruction so that a part of the factory could become productive again. There was the obvious damage from the bombs and the fighting and chaos that followed, but what the bombs didn't destroy, the Russians finished. They took away all the machines and what they did not take, they dismantled and destroyed. But as soon as the factory was operational again the former personnel were hired back. At first, staffing was on a part time basis but then gradually, as the factory became more productive, full time work began. I was called back early but for several months worked only two days a week. But then as the work became full time I had to find a solution for the care of my children. My mother was becoming too old to be a full-time babysitter, and the work in her garden and the care of the house were more than enough for her.

Monika and Rainer were already in school. But school was in the mornings and although it started early at eight am, by one o'clock school was out. There was a newly-opened daycare center nearby and I enrolled them for the afternoons. Irene was very young, but when I asked if they would take her as well, on a full time basis, they agreed as long as Irene was potty trained. Since Irene was potty-trained early, I could send her and felt relieved that Rainer and Monika would be able to join her for the afternoons.

Later as my work became more and more demanding, I often found myself working overtime, and needed to find more help at home. A young woman that I knew from my sports club days was looking for part-time house work and that was how Hanna came to work for me. She came when-ever it suited her own schedule to do housework, laundry, cooking and often would stay late when I worked overtime. She was grateful for the pay I could give and the extra foodstuffs I gave her helped to augment her ration cards.

There were so many things during the children's early years in Berlin that stick in my mind. The many little excursions that we took were always an adventure. Once when we went to visit Josef's aunt and uncle, Arthur and Elli, Josef decided that we should go on his motorcycle. So off we went, five people on one bike! Rainer was sitting in front of Josef on the gas tank, I was behind Josef with Monika on my lap, facing me, and on my back I carried little Irene, standing in a knapsack! When I think back to those times I wonder how we ever managed to get to our destination without an incident. Today of course there would be laws and ample policing to enforce that such foolish risks are not taken. But in those days, everything was improvised for we were all happy to have survived the war and post- war destruction, and happy to be able to engage in life.

We made trips without the children too. Grocery shopping trips into East Berlin were difficult. Berlin was divided into four different occupied zones, with four different types of occupation forces, and also two types of currency. The West-Mark had much more value than the Ost-Mark (East-Mark) with an exchange rate of one to four. It was much cheaper to buy our food staples in the East-sector, the Russian-Zone, and we often made these trips for vegetables which were really cheap, but they were the only commodity we could buy as nothing else was available there. A thriving black market resulted as all sorts of consumer goods were welcomed in the East. It was dangerous and it was always a gamble traveling from the West-Zone, the American sector where we lived, into the Russian-occupied zone because of the checkpoints between.

The most prominent checkpoint was "Check Point Charlie" on Friedrich Strasse, very near to where Potsdammer Platz had been bombed to rubble. We had a most memorable encounter with the *Volkspolizei*, the German police, who manned the checkpoint. Josef's friend, Georg, who lived in the East sector, offered us a kitchen stove. I was excited as I only had a two-ring hot plate, so an electric kitchen stove was very welcome. Off we went to the East Zone with our small older English car, a Dixie. Reluctantly Josef had traded his motor- cycle for the more practical car. There was no problem when we left the West sector and no great problem when we entered the East sector. We had the official permit of passage with all the necessary stamps and seals. But on the way back, with our stove stuffed into that little car, we were stopped, our car moved to a side-shed area, while we were detained aside. We were told that it was forbidden to take anything metal out of the East sector. We had paid for it in West-marks, but Georg had supplied us with a note saying it was a gift. It didn't matter, our car was searched. It was literally taken apart in that shed. We simply sat for several hours before we were allowed to get back to our car. Although now a wreck, it could still be driven, carefully, and we were allowed to leave, but without the stove.

There were many delays when entering the East Zone. We were told "you are approaching too fast, go back and come again slowly". Back we went only to approach the check point again, this time at a snail's pace and then told to wait, sometimes for an hour before being allowed to move again. But these were just minor incidents and inconveniences compared to the times in the recent past during the blockade, so we counted ourselves lucky.

Our home was full of life, and our life was very busy. Each day brought something new. One day when the children were quite young, I came home from work to find Monika's doll carriage hung around the chimney. It was not the doll carriage that I was worried about, it was *How on earth did the children manage to get it up on the roof?* It turned out that Winfried, my nephew, who was visiting, had that bright idea and with the children's collaboration put the thing there. Although I enjoyed my career, and we needed the income, it was at times like this that I felt guilty about my time away at work, and I worried constantly about the children.

On another day the children came home with a tiny kitten. They said they found it and did not know where it belonged, pleading to keep it. I, being an animal lover, said yes. Columbeene was an entertaining addition to our household that helped to teach the children the responsibility of taking care of a small being. One day Monika very excitedly told me that in her doll carriage were many small kittens. Columbeene had selected the doll carriage to have her babies in. Monika felt quite proud of them, they were "hers" and she wheeled the kittens around instead of her doll. That cat and her kittens was a prelude of more animal entertainment yet to come.

Josef came home from work one day with a field mouse in his lunch box. He had caught her during the day and thought it would make a nice meal for Columbeene. But when he took the mouse out and held it in the palm of his hand, intending to give it to Columbeene, the mouse instead of being afraid started to clean its whiskers. In an instant Josef decided to keep the little mouse as a pet. I had a large tin can that had held potatoes during the *Luftbruecke* and it made an ideal home for the mouse. In a short time the little mouse became so used to our hand that it became very tame. We would let it run loose on the table top where it would inquisitively sniff at everything, but when we knocked on the table top, it would come running back into our hand. This little mouse provided endless entertainment for us.

My mother borrowed the mouse one afternoon to show it to her 'coffee klatsh' visitors. She let it loose on the coffee table, and I could hear the shrieks of the little old church ladies all the way upstairs. But one knock on the table and it came back to mother's hand.

I even took the mouse to work. It traveled in my coat pocket, and felt right at home on my typewriter desk. Everyone was amazed when it returned back to my hand. My boss was so impressed with the mouse that he wanted to trade his Siamese cat, satin pillow and all, for the little mouse. I declined. We were very careful with the mouse when our cat was around, and at night the mouse, in its tin-can home, was locked up in the small closet we used as a storage room. The tin can was always covered with a large sieve strainer. One morning the mouse was not there. We looked and knocked, and could only assume that it must have become bold and jumped up until the sieve moved and it got out. Hoping that it would still be found we kept searching. That storage room was also where we kept the laundry basket. Next laundry day I found his little body. Stuck in the laundry, he had suffocated, leaving us with memories and appreciation of the entertaining gift that the mouse had shared with us.

Josef at this time was working in the ration break-down department of the American forces, a haven for mice, where he had caught "our" mouse. Luckily for us there was also a surplus of food which he also periodically brought home. I will never forget the evening when he brought home a large amount of donut dough. My mother ended up making donuts all night, and friends and neighbors found them- selves with gifts of donuts. But much of the food Josef brought home was used for barter. It was a food exchange that procured Irene's baby carriage and some nice baby clothes for her.

Soon the work at the ration break-down department came to an end, and Josef was again looking for work. My eldest half-sister (from my father's first marriage) had a husband, Willy, who worked as the head chef on the ocean liner named the Columbia. Josef had taken an extensive course in medical massage, medical water therapy, foot care and reflexology. This training and a good word from Willy landed Josef the job of orderly on the Colombia in the ship's medical office. This ship traveled between Bremerhaven and Quebec City and Montreal in Canada, and New York City in the United States. A round trip to the American continent and the lay-over time in the various ports took Josef away for three weeks at a time. Then came three days in Bremerhaven until the next trip started. Once again I became a traveling wife, and I traveled every three weeks the nearly 500km trip to Bremerhaven. Sometimes he was able to come home for a few days, but those times were rare.

Since my half sister, Herta lived there, I sometimes slept at her home, but sometimes I found myself at a hotel which only added to the already expensive cost of traveling. Then I found a unique way to travel to Bremerhaven. I managed to make arrangements with the milk trucks that traveled daily between West Berlin and Bremerhaven. That was the easy part. The difficulty was arranging time off from work, every three weeks! Overtime and much sympathy from my boss worked for a while, but finally he said "One day and no more". I had to think of something else. A taxi to the airport, a plane to Bremen and an arrangement with Josef to pick me up by car at the Bremen airport. Then drive 100km to Bremerhaven, spend the night and return via the same route the next morning. I was so lucky that my mother agreed to look after the children while I was away on these visits. Our stays together often became parties with his shipmates and their spouses. My three weeks of routine was punctuated with excitement on these short weekend trips, and memories were built!

While the Columbia was in layover in Quebec, Montreal and New York, the crew went ashore to explore and shop. Josef used that time to learn as much as possible about the land and its people. It helped that the ship-board nurse on the Columbia, Nurse Anneliese, had friends in Montreal. Josef became friends with the family, and there was much discussion around the dinner table about the economy and political climate in Canada. It was during these times that the idea of immigrating to Canada was born. The idea became more concrete every time Joe came home to Berlin.

The cramped living arrangements in my mother's small two story- house proved to be more and more challenging. The tiny upstairs that we called our apartment was only two small rooms with an additional third room that was used a kitchen. Of the two little rooms, one was a living room by day and became our bedroom at night. We squeezed in the beds for all three of the children in the other tiny room. The apartment was tolerable as long as the children were babies, but when Irene was also of school age, it was just too small for five people. It helped that we had the use of the large garden, but the sleeping arrangements were always a puzzle. The downstairs of the house was occupied by my mother, my sister Lisa, and my youngest sister Carin. The turbulent times after the war were difficult for everyone. My sister Christa was married briefly and had a son, Martin who was born February 5,1951. He was three years younger than my youngest, Irene and when Christa's marriage broke up she too came to live in that small house with her son. The house was full. Although Christa eventually went to London, England to find work, her son remained with us until she could find ways and means to get settled in her new country. London was in worse shape than Berlin as they too had suffered terrible bomb damage. But Berlin was luckier than London: at least there was some rebuilding going on as the allies had a keen interest in keeping West Berlin going because of its strategic location within Russian territories.

Living arrangements were relieved a little during the time Josef was away travelling the ocean, as he was gone for three weeks at a time, but soon the Columbia, which was a very old ship, was taken out of commission and scrapped. Josef, unemployed again, was back living full time in that crowded house.

You may think, why not move? Well, where could we move to? Berlin was 70% destroyed with available living space at a premium. Re-building had just begun, but Berlin was an island city in Russian territory and the only expansion was up. Everyone who had accommodations was to stay where they were with priority obviously given to others. We had a place to stay so we were on the bottom of a wait- ing list for larger quarters.

There were other pressures too. Once when I was shopping for bread in the local corner store, the store owner called me by my last name, Frau Koenigsberger. At that point another customer muttered under his breath, but clearly audible; "I guess the Nazis didn't get them all", Koenigsberger being a Jewish-sounding name. We applied for immigration to Canada.

PHOTOGRAPHS

German paper money. 1910

Hertha (Auguste) Wegner, WWI Field Nurse, 1918

Hertha (Auguste) Wegner, WWI Field Nurse, 1918

August Gutzeit, WWI Cavalry Officer, 12th Lancers Regiment of Insterburg - (watercolor painting by fellow officer Hans Scrhramm).

Dorothea's parents wedding. Hertha (Auguste) Wegner and August Gutzeit. 1920

Dorothea's maternal grandparents Anorte Plorinn 1865-1936 & Friedrich Wegner 1870-1945

Maternal grandparents homestead in Lucknojen (Neuenrode) East Prussia. 1904

Dorothea. 6 months, with her mother Hertha, 1921.

Dorothea age 2 ½ years with Lisa 7 months, 1923.

Dorothea (with bow) Hertha with Lisa, Frieda and August. 1926

Lisa, Dorothea (standing) with Christa and Gerd.

Berlin house, as it looked in 1999.

Dorothea. Confirmation photo, age 13, 1934

Dorothea with father August aboard the Bremen, 1935

Dorothea aboard the Bremen, 1935

Ahlbeck, Baltic Sea (kayaking trip cut short, noting German war ships, and declaration of war) 1939

Soldiers as well as young Arbeitsdienst men, including Herbert (later he became Sergeant in the Artillery) 1939

At the Arbeitsdienst, 1939

Herbert on left, Dorothea on right.

Hitler salute begins the work day.

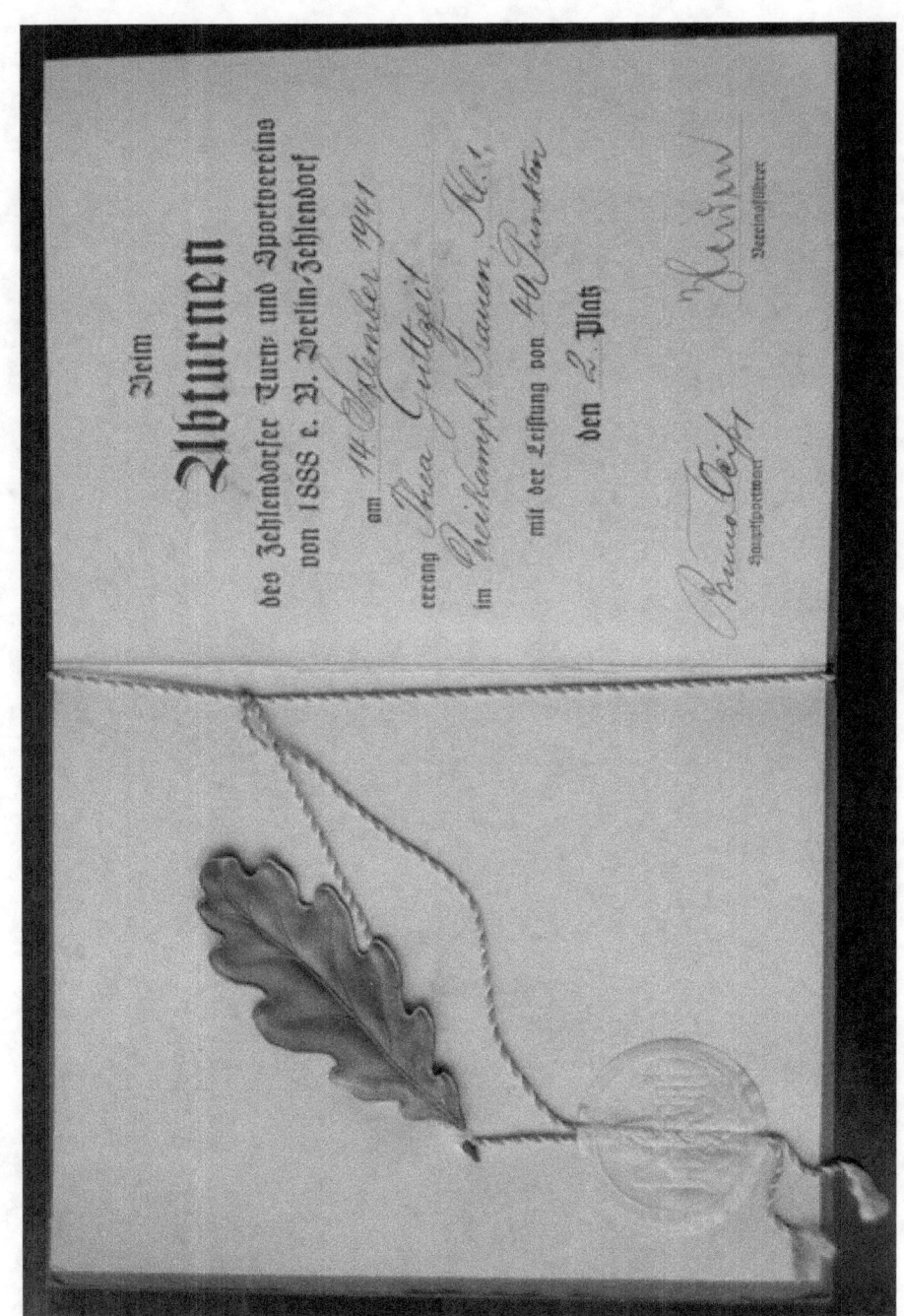

Sports club 1934 – 1940.

Dorothea sitting.

Dorothea. Wedding Oct 24, 1942

Bottom: Wedding guests, left to right:

1	Lisa Gutzeit, (Dorothea's sister)	9	Else (Herbert's mother)
2	Otto Stimming (Herbert's paternal grandfarther)	10	Dorothea
3	Helen Stimming (Herbert's paternal grandmother)	11	Herbert
4	Elizabeth Keller (Herbert's maternal grandmother)	12	Hertha (Dorothea's mother)
5	A girlfriend of Dorothea's (head down in photo)	13	A girlfriend of Dorothea's
6	Christa Gutzeit (white dress, Dorothea's sister)	14	Carin Gutzeit, girl (Dorothea's sister)
7	Kaethe (Herbert's aunt)	15	Whilem (Herbert's father)
8	Kaethe's husband	16	Werner (Herbert's brother)
		17	Erika (Herbert's sister)

Dorothea, Rainer and Monika 1945

Monika and Rainer, well-fed on a diet of horse oats, 1945.

Dorothea's work register 1935 - 1949

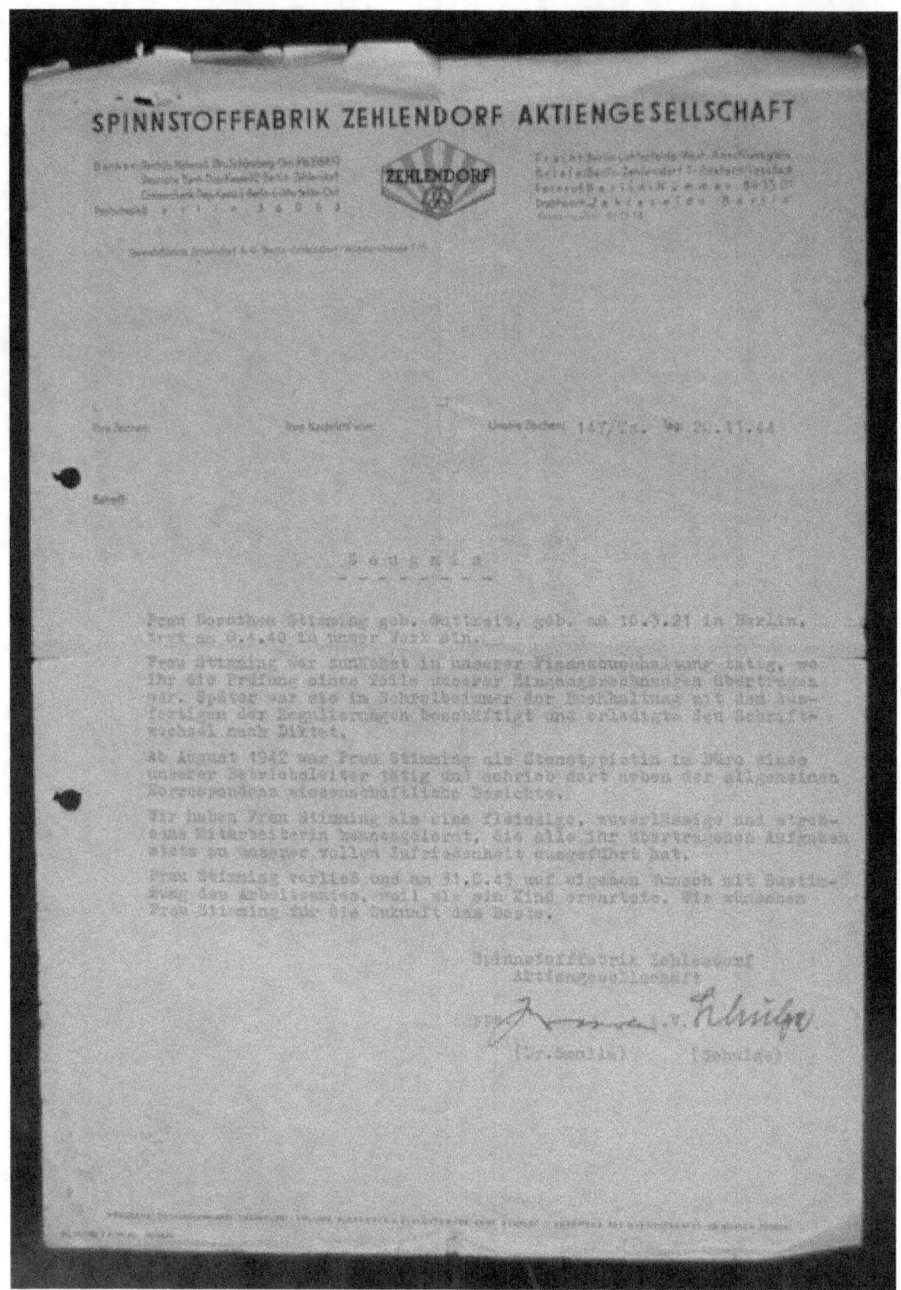

Spinnstofffabrik (nylon factory where Dorothea worked). 1944

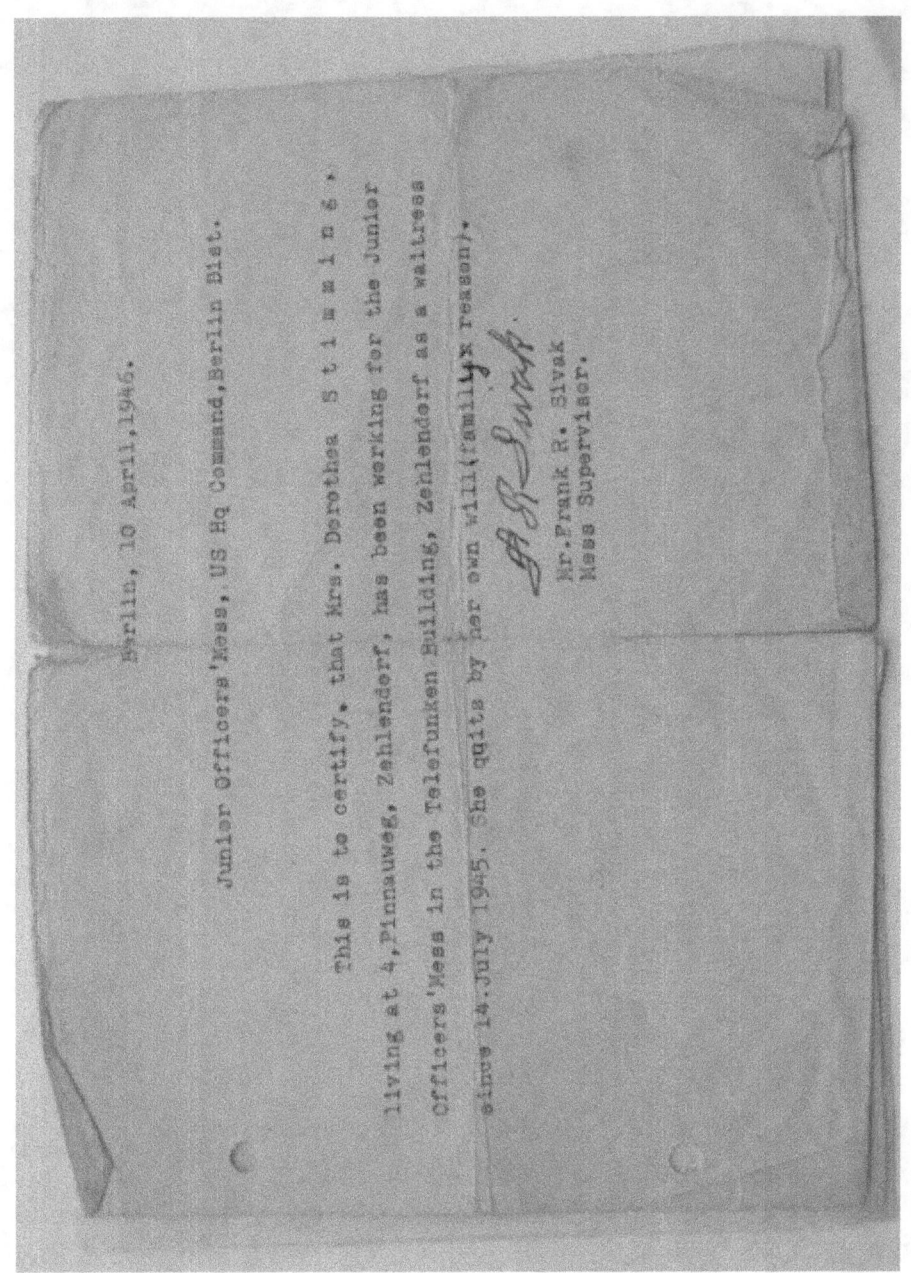

Berlin, 10 April,1946.

Junior Officers'Mess., US Hq Command,Berlin Dist.

This is to certify, that Mrs. Dorothea S t i m m i n g .,
living at 4,Pinnauweg, Zehlendorf, has been working for the Junior
Officers'Mess in the Telefunken Building, Zehlendorf as a waitress
since 14.July 1945. She quits by her own will(family reason).

Mr.Frank R. Sivak
Mess Supervisor.

U.S. Junior Officers' Mess note concerning Dorothea leaving her job. 1946

Berlin ruins, 1945
Top: Kreuzung Unter den Linden / Friedrichstrasse Crossroads.
Bottom: Alye Bibliothek am Bebelplaz. The Old Library on the Bebelplaz

Baby Josef and his mother Martha 1923

Josef in school photo (black shirt in center) 1930

Haus Vaterland am Potsdamer Platz, 1930s The entire area destroyed during WWII.

Josef age 17. 1940

Dorothea and Josef 1947

Josef and fellow workers at the Telefunken American Army base 1947-1948

The Columbia ocean liner Josef worked on. 1952.

Dorothea and Josef with Rainer, Monika and baby Irene 1948

Last Christmas celebration in Berlin, one week before Dorothea and children left for Canada, 1954
Left to right: Monika, partial view Carin, speaking with Hertha
Hertha (Dorothea and Carin's mother) Ziggi (Carin's husband, standing) Freda, standing
Children
Martin on Hertha's (Oma) lap Ingrid, standing behind candles Rainer
Irene, on her father Josef's lap Josef and Dorothea

CANADA

Joe's first car in Canada, a1949 Buick. 1955

Joe and customer at their restaurant 1965

Their motel. 1976

The old farm house in Warkworth; the renovations were to be Dorothea and Joe's retirement project. - 1906

The old farm house in Warkworth; the renovations were to be Dorothea and Joe's retirement project. - 1987

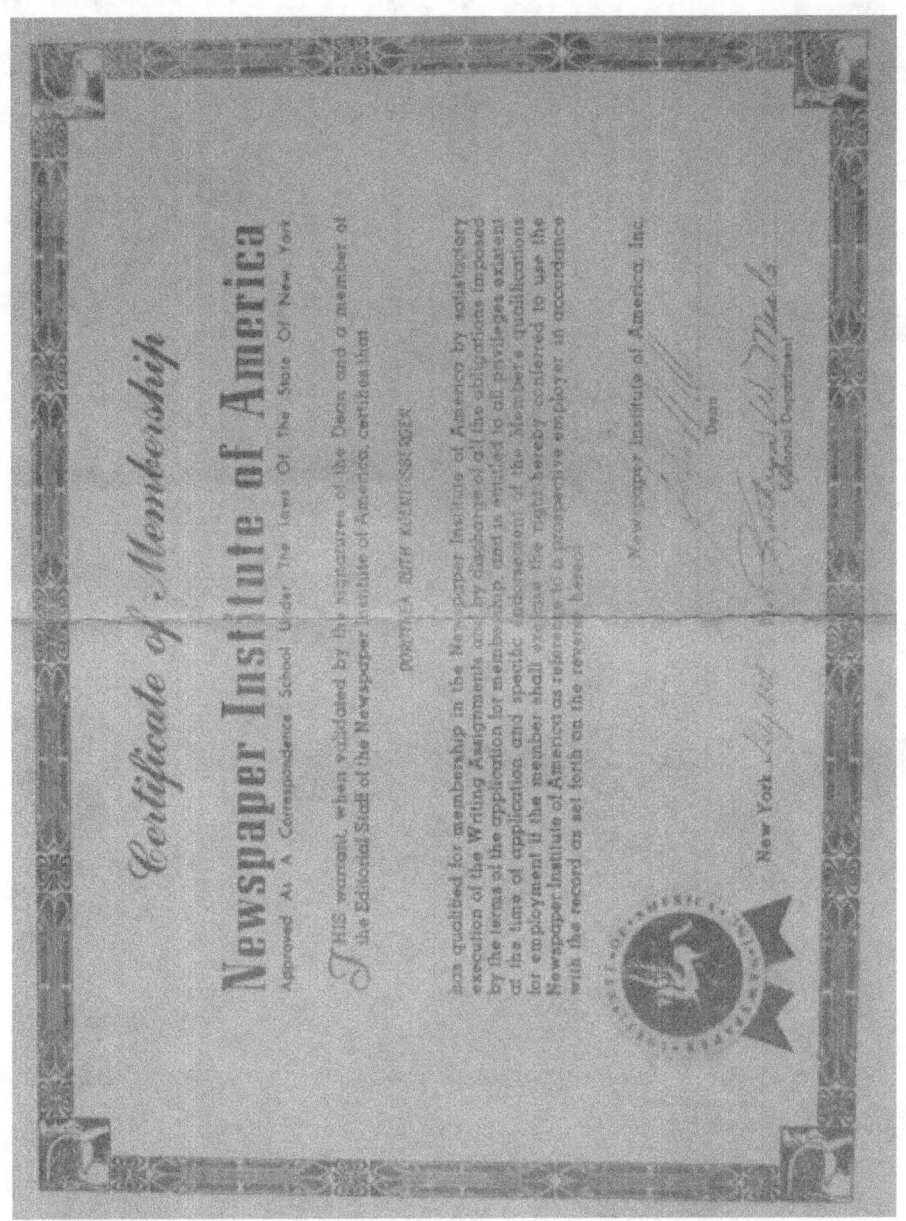

Dorothea's Newspaper Institute of America certificate. 1979

With a winning speech entitled "Power and Glory," Thea Koenigsberger was the outstanding speaker during the First Oshawa Toastmistress Club annual speech contest. Thea will now go on to compete in the Council Two speech contest being held on April 9 at the Deerhurst Inn, Huntsville. First runner-up in the contest was Jean Holtom, and second runner-up was Sandy Cunningham.
—Times photo

Oshawa Times, 1983
maple sugar, rock maple, striped maple, sugar maple. Michaux, F.A., The North American
Sylva, vol. 1: t. 43 (1817-1819)

Pl. 43.

Black Sugar Maple.
Acer nigrum

H.J. Redouté plantillustrations.org/illustration.php?id_illustration=158502

PART 2

CANADA

1955 - 2005

The Sugarbush Cottage in Canada that Dorothea and Josef built. 1980

FIVE

1955 - 1969

Immigration and a new future

Considering all the paperwork and the many certificates necessary for the immigration applications, it took a surprisingly short time — five months, and Josef had a visa for Canada. It was July 1955 when he boarded an ocean liner heading to Montreal. Having traveled this ocean route many times before, made the trip routine, except for the hopes and apprehensions that this trip would deliver him to a new life in a new land, with new challenges, strange ways and even a new language. But determination to make a better life kept Josef's spirits buoyant.

Upon arriving at the port of Montreal and immediately after pass- ing through the immigration's reception, Josef was anxious to get started in the right direction for his new life. He purchased a train ticket for Vancouver, but before leaving Montreal he contacted the family he had befriended while on his previous ocean voyages. They told him of possible work that was available in Oshawa, Ontario and forewarned him that finding work in Vancouver could be difficult. They advised him to change his train ticket, which he did, happy for the extra money that was returned to him. Vancouver, he found out, was certainly a much longer journey than to Oshawa, Ontario. This new country was vast and later, after many years in Canada, Josef still marveled at the distances within Canada's boundaries.

Josef arrived in Oshawa at 7:00 am on the morning of a very hot and humid day in July. When he stepped off the train-station plat- form the long street before him shimmered with a heat that quickly changed his mind about walking to downtown, and he hailed a taxi. Not wanting to waste any time, Josef asked the driver to show him around the city, the factories, the bank; and first things first, asked the driver to take him to the employment office. It was too early and with the office not yet open, Josef invited the cab driver for a coffee. Not intending to dampen Josef's spirits, the driver told Josef that it would be hard to get a job at General Motors; the city's main employ- er, was on a prolonged strike. Everyone there was scrambling for work.

Without hesitation, Josef told the taxi driver that when he was in Montreal, he had heard that molders were sought after in Oshawa, which factory could that be? The taxi driver stated that there was only one foundry in Oshawa called ' The Fittings'. "Please take me to it", was Josef's demand. Josef marched into the factory's main office and asked for the personnel 'chef'. "What do you want?" was the question posed back to Josef. "Work; I heard that you hire molders", replied Josef.

It must have been quite a scene in that office with Josef's insistence spoken loud and clear in his very broken English with a heavy German accent. But the response was favorable, "That's right. Can you be here at 1:00 and start the afternoon shift?" came the reply.

Then came the questions and necessary paperwork that had to be filled out. When it came to the question of address, where does Josef live, he excused himself stating "please wait a moment" and rushed out to the waiting taxi driver. Josef told the driver that he needed a room and an address in a hurry, would the driver be aware of any room for rent. To which the driver replied "You are lucky again, I happen to have one available." The driver gave Josef a card with his address on it and left, leaving Josef to finish filling in the application at the Fittings personnel office.

Having completed the forms, Josef found that he had very little time before he had to report back and begin work at 1:00. He hailed another taxi and asked to be taken to the address on the card the first driver had given him.

Josef rushed to his new address and surprised the woman who answered the door. She watched in astonishment when Josef asked with anxious haste to be shown to his room. Her taxi driver husband had not yet returned from his work to inform her that the room was rented. With much explaining, in limited and accented English, Josef was able to convince her and was eventually led to an upstairs guest room. A quick change into working clothes, another taxi ride and Josef reported to work, punctually at 1:00 sharp. He had been in Canada 24 hours and only 6 hours since his arrival in Oshawa!

Those first days passed with bewildering speed, and it was not until Josef received his first pay check that he was able breathe a sigh of relief with profound appreciation, thankful heart and hope for a future.

The work at Fittings Ltd. was not easy. He started as a molder doing piece work; then he went on to do a variety of different jobs, including feeding a huge oven with shovels full of special sand to be melted. Eventually he managed to acquire a job on the electrical run of the production line. His electrical training in the Germany military, along with a good word from a new-found friend, enabled him to land the job that looked after the ' line' that feeds the band for the molds. Josef was always able to make friends and talk with strangers, sharing laughter and ideas. Soon his friends shortened his name to Joe and it stuck for the rest of his life. Still it was tough work, but Joe was feeling settled enough to start looking for accommodations suit- able to allow me and the children to come to Canada and join him.

His efforts were futile as no landlord wished to rent to a family with three children. Being German did not help either, as the war was still fresh in everyone's mind. Joe saw little alternative and saved and scraped enough money together for a down payment on a small house that was for sale in a working-class neighborhood. It was located on a short street across from a trucking company and behind that ran the railway tracks. The house itself was actually a converted cottage with a small loft upstairs and a closed front porch. It had a basement that housed a coal furnace and water heater, and had a little storage room partitioned off to one side. Without any other choice, Joe was able to visualize potential, and here in the basement he fixed a room for him- self and rented out the rest. Soon I received a letter telling me that the children and I could follow him to Canada.

Now began a busy time for me. I was still working long hours at the *Spinne* and had to squeeze in time off to allow for the many appointments in order to get all the necessary immigration papers for the children and myself. Then there were health tests for all of us and immunizations to get. Packing was another challenge. What to take and what to leave behind? I managed to get three wooden crates from the *Spinne*. These were the crates used for the export of nylon and rayon thread. Since the boxes were only three feet high, four feet long and only two-and-a-half feet wide, some big decisions had to be made as to what I really wanted to take with us. These three crates along with three suitcases and a two-foot square wicker basket, which carried our linens and clothes, was all I was to bring with me to Canada. Incidentally that wicker basket had quite a history. My mother took it with her to the Russian front when she was nursing during the first World War. Later the basket housed her 'things' after her marriage, and then it was used for extra storage space in that tiny house in Berlin. Now it was to make the long journey to Canada where I would use it for most of my life, until I finally moved to a retirement home.

During the busy activity of preparing to go to Canada and join Joe, my mind was constantly fretting. Our marriage up to now had been a turbulent one, full of excitement, frustration and anxiety - which first led to thoughts about not going. Then I had thoughts about the mess and huge changes that a move to Canada would make of everyone's lives. Among all the thoughts running through my mind, one thought was paramount, Joe was a good father, a good provider and a good man. I realized a lot of the frustrations came from the legacy of the war and then any anxious thoughts about not going left me as quickly as they had come. Of course I would go.

Now I began to fret about what I would find in Canada. Other than the trips of my youth, I had never lived in any other house than my mother's. This was home and I was leaving it, my family, but also my country, to go to a new land. I was worrying over so many things: Would my children fit in? How would their school grades compare? Would their limited English be good enough or would they have to repeat grades? Would my English be good enough to find a decent job? Was Joe able to get beds for all of us? What about chairs and a table. The questions plaguing my mind were endless.

Time quickly flashed by and soon it was November 23, 1955 and my children and I started on our long journey. With a heavy heart I left my mother and my sisters knowing that my life would never be the same. But my hopes for our future and a better life for my children, gave me all the courage I needed to quiet my fears. Surely nothing would ever be as difficult and dreadful as the war years. And Canada was politically stable with an optimistic economic outlook.

The children and I boarded a bus for Bremerhaven. The trip through the Soviet Zone (East

Germany) was punctuated by numerous stops as our papers and luggage were constantly being checked and re- checked. Finally we arrived in Bremerhaven where my half-sister, Herta and her husband were waiting for us. They assisted us in boarding the ocean liner, the "Seven Seas", and waved us off. That first night we settled in the rather cramped third-class dormitory accommodations. Too tired to care we simply shut out the noises and tried to get some much-needed sleep. The next day, much to my delight, my brother-in-law, Willy, the retired kitchen master from the ocean liner "Columbia", through his connections, had our accommodation upgraded, and for the remainder of the ocean voyage we had a first class cabin all to ourselves! And what a good thing this was, because all three children were seasick for most of the journey starting before the ship had even left the river Elbe! Rainer never forgot that. The food served on the voyage was absolutely delicious, and that first night he had to miss cabbage rolls, one of his favorite meals. I felt fine and aside from looking after the children, I was free to enjoy the luxury and comfort of the modern ship.

The voyage was uneventful, aside from the one moment of excitement when an iceberg was observed in the distance, and then the one quiet night when the engines were turned off for minor repairs. Then on December 5, 1955 we arrived in Canada to find a cold and snowy landscape awaiting us. Fortunately we landed in Quebec City fully rested as all our energy was going to be required for the next leg of the journey. In Quebec we had to go through the lengthy immigration procedures and by the time we boarded the train to Montreal we were all exhausted. In Montreal it was another long wait for the connecting train to Oshawa. Finally came the long all-night train ride with little Irene being the only one able to get some sleep as she lay stretched out on the hard wooden benches. It should be noted that it wasn't until shortly after our trip that railway cars were upgraded with up- holstered seats.

Traveling through the night and arriving in Oshawa at 7:10 AM in the still dark of the winter night, we disembarked with all our luggage. There I stood, on the empty platform with my children in hand, and no Joe there to greet us. I cannot begin to describe the torrent of feelings that were silently crushing me!

At the little booth beside the platform, I found the station-master and this is when I discovered that there were two train stations in Oshawa, the Pacific Railway line and the National Railway line, with trains arriving from Montreal half an hour apart. Joe was at the wrong station because the telegram I had sent to him, advising him of our arrival time, did not specify which railway line we would be on. So we waited on the cold dark station platform until Joe came.

That first day at our new home was a blur. After a quick welcome and a hurried ride to our house, Joe immediately left again for work as he could not afford to miss a single day. And here I was, in my new home in Canada! The children dropped on their beds totally exhausted as I began to familiarize myself with the small house.

To make ends meet, Joe had rented out the main floor, which consisted of three rooms, a living room, bedroom and kitchen, to a young couple. The upstairs loft, which was divided with a curtain into two very small rooms, was to be the children's bedrooms. The follow- ing year when times were again lean, and we were to rent out one section of the loft to another new German immigrant for six months. But for now the kids slept upstairs and that left the basement for our use. There Joe had made a makeshift kitchen complete with a large sink and sectioned-off small area for a bedroom, and the rest of the basement housed the furnace and coal. Everything seemed in disarray. Feeling disillusioned, disappointed and tired, I used what energy I had left and through my silent tears, I started to unpack the few belongings that we had brought with us. I began organizing the small house so that it started to look like a home. By the time Joe came back from work things began to look and feel a bit less strange. We had beds, but the table was accompanied by wooden crates tipped on their ends to use a chairs. I quickly covered these with my precious linens that I had brought. Then, after a simple supper, Joe and I left to buy some staples. I had brought $40 with me and now, with all the money that was left over after our journey, Joe drove me shopping before I could finally fall into bed. I had been in Canada not quite two days, with half the time spent on the train, on a wooden seat and now settling in that strange place I was to call home. But we were here, together, in Oshawa, Canada with Joe.

Joe had used his few months in Canada well. After work, at the German club he had befriended several new immigrant Germans. Among these was Carl-Heinz, an active and fun loving motor mechanic. Heinz was a few years younger than Joe, and together these two had many adventures. One of the first was to find Joe an old but reliable car. It was with great pride that Joe took me on that first shopping trip in his own American car. Together with Carl-Heinz they had repaired it to relatively good working order. Buying a car was one of Joe's first priorities, even before the house, as he had quickly realized that here in Canada, with the long distances between everywhere, one would be lost without a car. Just getting to work required a car.

With all the effort and anxiety of this first day my emotions were tight, but I was proud of myself and the way I was able to hold "it" together. But when my nylon stockings, that I had so carefully cared for, tore on a piece of rusted metal on the side of the car as I stepped in, I burst into loud sobs! I hadn't yet realized that, while nylon stockings were a luxury, difficult and expensive to obtain in Germ- any; here in Canada you could buy them in any grocery store!

Still thinking about the very limited supplies we had in Germany, it was a delightful surprise to see the different groceries and produce available at the food store. I filled the shopping cart, also something new to me. In Germany we picked out our purchases, placing them in the cloth shopping tote-bags that we brought with us, then we laid them out to be counted, then re-packed the goods in those same bags to carry home.

As the stove and 'real' kitchen was in the rented out part of our house, I again had to learn to cook on a two-burner hot plate. A good thing I had learned *turm-cooking* (tower cooking) after the war when the electricity was often not available. Tower cooking meant putting one pot on top of the other. But one had to watch and change the pots to make the food come out evenly cooked. It was fortunate that Joe and the children liked "one-pot" dishes, such as stews, soups and chili. Later, when I worked again, I used another cooking technique that I had learned during the war when it became necessary to cook while conserving the rationed electricity. We called it the *koch- kiste* (cook-box). I would put a feather comforter in a box and I lined it further with a feather pillow, then a large towel. As soon as the food on the burner started to boil, I would put the pot on the towel in the feather cushion, and covered it well. The food would continue cooking until I was ready to take it out. The food could be in that feather bed cook-box without ever burning or being overcooked. I think this was an original crock-pot idea!

My first day in Canada had been exhausting. It wasn't just the physical rearranging and unpacking, it was the emotions of finally being in my new environment, and the finality of leaving Berlin and my home behind, that took its emotional toll. After a long, deep sleep, I awoke ready to face my second day in Oshawa, which turned into an equally busy one. First I enrolled the children in school. Monika and Rainer, after a brief exam, were put into grade six, the same grade they were in Berlin. Irene, who had not had English classes in Berlin, started back in Grade one, even though she had finished it in Berlin. In Germany the school year starts after the Easter break in spring, not the fall as it does here. Irene was the only one who balked at starting school so quickly, so she didn't start school until her third day in Canada. Even the children were caught in the hectic pace to get on with our new life, a pace that continued for several years as we worked to get established.

After the school business I went to the employment office. It was necessary for me to work to make ends meet. Joe's wages were $65 a week, the mortgage payment was $65 a month; with the car, insurance, and utility bills there was not much left for food or anything else. As well, in the beginning we still had many household things that were missing and somehow had to be bought. We needed some furniture and the children needed Canadian clothes. The clothes they came in, from Berlin, made them stand out among their classmates, and I do not have to explain what that means.

The interview at the employment office went well, until they asked how long I had been in Canada. I had to say one day. The interviewing lady laughed and said come back in a month or so. I never did get a job through the employment office. I always found work by myself, although it took some time.

Joe and I experienced some worrisome times until Joe, by word- of-mouth heard that an elderly lady, who lived almost across the street from us, was looking for some help. She was diabetic and required a companion to sleep at her home during the night as she became fearful and did not wish to be alone. I went over to inquire about the terms and what was expected. I was hired to come over between 8:00 and 9:00pm, stay the night in her antique furnished guest room, and then give her the insulin injection in the morning. The pay was $10 a week. As we needed the money, I went, but continued searching the newspapers for a real job.

I knew I had better learn Canadian English, as the English I had learned in Berlin would not get me an office job here. I figured the best way to learn was to get a job as a waitress and converse with all sorts of people. Soon I found a job in a small restaurant where I worked 9 to 5, then went home to my family and returned to the lady at 9:00PM. I was busy; working, preparing family meals, the lady … but there is always a silver lining. The restaurant I was working in catered to the General Motors workers in a battery plant that was situated across the street from it, and hence was closed on Saturday and Sunday. This arrangement left those two days free for me to spend with my family, and slowly but surely we settled into a sort of routine.

But this was short lived. Along with the already tight finances, there were some upheavals in our household. One that I vividly remember was when the old house's foundation, which was made of fieldstone and mortar, required repair. The mortar between the stones had become brittle, and when our first spring in Oshawa came, so did the water. Tiny rivulets sneaked through the mortar. A very uncomfortable situation since our basement was also our kitchen and bedroom. But we had no money to fix it. Then Joe had an idea. The whole family was encouraged to chew gum which we then plugged into the tiny cracks. For a week we chewed, and Joe plugged the cracks every time a new one was found. It worked, for a while at least. Then the toilet became blocked. But Joe, with the help of one of his friends, was able to solve that problem. Since the house only had one toilet, for us and the renters, it was crucial to keep it operational. Then the furnace broke and before that first spring was up we had to install a new one.

We had no option but to go to a finance company for a loan, and try to negotiate the lowest interest possible. It took several years to pay back that loan. Buying on loan was totally new to us, but the pressure of payments was also not lost. We vowed to, if at all possible, never borrow again, except for the house mortgage of course, and that was to be paid off as quickly as possible.

The last misfortune of that first spring was that our new pet cat, which had been given to the children by a friend of Joe's, had become very sick. She started a very peculiar behavior, and was running in circles and even running against the wall. We quickly realized that she had distemper and had to be put down. Of course we couldn't afford veterinary bills, and while I sent the children away on an errand, once again, a friend helped us with this unpleasant necessity.

Finally that first spring was over and with it came some changes in our routine that were to keep us busy on the weekends as well. Joe found a construction job, and he began working there on Saturday and Sundays. I read in the paper that a farmer in Whitby, just west of Oshawa was looking for help picking strawberries. The children and I decided to go there on Saturday morning. Joe drove us the night before to show us where this farm was and luckily it was a direct route, right on Highway #2. Still used to the way we walked or bicycled everywhere in Berlin, we set off to walk to the farm. Driving the night before with Joe, the farm did not seem to be too far. But not realizing the great distances in Canada, it is not surprising that after a three hour walk we were too tired, and it was too hot at mid-day to pick berries. The farmer felt for us, offered us some berries to eat with the lunch we brought and then he drove us back home.

We found that Rainer had a strawberry allergy, so berry picking was out for him. He found a paper route to work. Little Irene, wanting to help too, continued to come berry picking with me, once we had arranged a ride. It was a blessing that Monika had homemaker instincts and was a terrific help at home. Otherwise I would not have been able to work those many hours and days. We were all busy seven days a week just to keep afloat. It was meal times, and those evenings with friends that kept us sane. The simple meals, music, conversation and games formed a bond between friends who became like an extended family.

So it came to be that on those two weekend days, while Joe worked construction, I went picking whatever was in season: straw- berries, raspberries, tomatoes and apples. A ride was arranged to collect us in Oshawa and drive to the fields. We worked for eight hours for our wages, then one more hour for the car ride. We were paid $1:00 an hour, but somehow it helped with our finances! It was extremely hard work, bending and lifting, which eventually ruined my back; I paid dearly for that with much pain as I got older. These weekend jobs continued for three summers, even on into a time when I had an office job to replace the waitress work.

We became friends with the farmer and his family, and on our first Christmas in Canada he showed up at our house with a bottle of cheer. Along with the warmth and laughter Joe decided to share some cheer with one of our new pets. And that's quite a story!

At Joe's work, at the Fittings Co. special sand was imported for the moldings. Joe found a snake in the molding sand and being an animal lover, decided to bring it home rather than have it destroyed. It was a small snake no bigger than a large milkshake straw. From a second -hand shop we obtained a beautiful wicker flower-box stand lined with tin. It was a large rectangle box held up by four long legs. Joe made a wooden frame for the top and screened it in, fastening it shut with a hook and latch. We put sand into it and the snake had a new home. But what to feed it? In the basement was a large sink, and that is where we had some minnows that were supposed to feed the snake. That first Christmas, Joe was so happy with the unexpected visit of the farmer that he decided to share the cheer a little further, and poured some for the fish. Next morning a sober Joe felt bad that the fish were floating so he held them between his fingers and moved them back and forth in the water hoping to re-activate their gills. I'm not sure if he felt bad for the fish, the snake or his pocket book as the minnows would have to be replaced.

The snake would not eat so Joe inquired at a pet store and was informed that snakes usually eat only live food. We tried the live minnows, earthworms and even tried tying a piece of meat on a string from the screen lid. Then when anyone passed the cage, we would pull on the string to make the food wiggle. Nothing worked and eventually the snake starved to death. Joe took the snake to the pet store and when the store owner took a look at it and checked, he informed Joe that he was very, very lucky. The molding sand had been import- ed from a tropical desert, and this snake was a poisonous sand viper!

This story carried through to Joe's work and friends. Carl-Heinz, Joe's friend, thought this was so hilarious, not that the snake was poisonous, but that Joe's family actually liked the snake! One Saturday afternoon he arrived with an obviously full paper shopping bag. He opened up the bag and tossed something on the kitchen floor. I was peeling potatoes and got such a fright when a huge garter snake slithered out, that I dropped one of the potatoes. The snake stretched forward and swallowed the potato in one gulp. The men laughed, but were very quick to gather the sluggish monster and dispose of it far away in a field. I was not impressed!

Our whole family loved animals, and we had many varied pets. Once someone gave the children two rabbits. They were fully grown, probably more than a year or two old. As we were told that they were both male, I agreed to let the children keep them. We had an old tool shed in the back yard, and this made a perfect rabbit hutch. Much to our surprise, we discovered one day that there were young with the rabbits. Unfortunately they did not live long. The rabbits, who we now understood were a couple, were in fact very old, too old to have healthy babies.

Then a short time later the female was dead too. That left the large rust-colored male alone. One day someone left the hutch door open, and it escaped. But it did not wander far, and stayed on the backyard lawn, just happy to have its freedom. We felt it should have more time outside its small hutch, but had to make sure it did not get into the neighbor's garden. We had a fence all along the back and on one side of the yard, with one side completely open. And that was the side where the neighbor had a full vegetable garden. Joe stooped down, took Rusty by his long ears, and walked the length of the open side of our yard, all the while telling him how far he could go. Would you believe it, Rusty never left our back yard! But he learned to climb up the porch stairs and wait at the back door for one of us to come out. One day Joe let him into the house and from then on it became a routine. Joe was home from work early in the afternoon every day before either the children or I came back. When we arrived it was always the same. There on the couch was Joe with the rabbit, stretched legs to the front and back, lying right beside him. Rusty loved sitting on your lap and being petted. He was wonderful company, for a rabbit.

And there were other pets. I came home from work one day to find that Irene had a shoe box, and in it she had brought home two small white rats from school. The fifth grade children had them in the class room as a project, and the teacher was looking for a place where they could be kept over the summer holidays. Irene volunteered, and here they were. They found a home in that tin-lined flower box that had in earlier days been home for that poor little starving snake. Naturally the little rats did not go back to school after the holidays, and they lived with us to be very old rats indeed. Luckily they were of the same sex, as we never had little ones to entertain us, but entertain us these rats surely did!

Our table was a busy place, often the children played games or colored, and I would sit by it to knit or sew. The rats were allowed to run around freely on the table investigating everything on it. One day I was sitting by the table mending while watching the rats playing in and around the sewing box. I was still a smoker at this time and parked my cigarette in the ashtray. When I wanted to pick it up again, it was gone. The rats had dragged it into their flower-box home which was lined with cotton balls and wood shavings. Afraid of a fire I frantically searched their home, but soon realized that the cigarette would have stopped burning as soon as the rats bit holes into it when they were pulling it. They sat there sniffing at the cold cigarette, so I lit another one and blew smoke into their faces. The rats went ecstatic, standing up and literally inhaling the smoke! They loved the nicotine smell, and from then on they enjoyed a cigarette with me.

It wasn't just the pets that added life and happiness to our home. My sister Christa, her husband George and their two children followed our immigration to Canada. They stayed with us for a short period of time and soon had a place of their own. It was wonderful to have extended family in Canada, in the same city. Little Martin who had stayed with us in our Berlin home for a while quickly became friends with Irene again. She was just a couple of years older and proudly showed him her Canadian English. But a real delight was Christa and George's new baby, Karin, who was just a few months old.

It was around this time that an opportunity arose, and we were sponsored to send our children to a Kiwanis summer camp. Just like the Lutheran summer camps I had been to in my youth, I felt that this would be a great opportunity and experience for my children. Rainer came home sunburned, dirty but happy. Not so for Irene. After only a few days of the two-week camp we went to visit and were advised that Irene had spent most of the time crying; she did not feel up to joining the other children and missed her home. Needless to say, we took her home with us.

After a year working in the restaurant I was hired by a small down- town hotel as a receptionist. This was an improvement in wages, and I finally had a typewriter under my fingers again. As there were also late shifts, four to midnight, I had to give up my job with the elderly lady. Monika took over going at night to the lady's house, and I went there only in the morning to give the lady her insulin. Even later Irene took over this job too, but one day I received a frantic call at the hotel from Irene. She could not get the lady to answer the door. Irene could hear the television, and when she climbed on the porch railing to peer into the window at the top of the door, she noticed the lady lying on the floor. I suggested to Irene, who was only twelve at the time, to go next door where there was a little store still open, and wait. I arrived shortly with the ambulance and police. This job ended as the lady never recovered from the stroke she had suffered and was dead not three weeks later. It was a sad event, but very much part of life itself.

As a hotel receptionist, I felt as if I was back working in a "real" office, but a year and a half later, when I found a job with a lawyer in Whitby, I knew I really had an office job again. I landed this job be- cause the lawyer's secretary, a German lady, was willing to train me in the legal business. For five years I commuted from Oshawa to Whitby, which in those days was a rather long commute, from one city to another. I worked part-time at first, then three years full-time for the princely sum of $50 a week. But I learned.

It was during this time that my eldest daughter Monika got married. We were barely four years in Canada and struggling, but with friends and careful planning, were able to have a wonderful wedding. I was concerned, as she was young, but we were ecstatic when her first daughter Liz was born, then a year and a bit later, came her second daughter Gabe. My first grandchildren were lively and a treasure to be with. My only regret is that my life was so full and busy, that the time with the grandchildren was short and went by far too quickly.

Five years in Canada and so much had happened. Then Joe received news that his mother had passed. We had no phone and mail was slow. Three weeks had passed before he received that dreadful letter. My heart was heavy for him as he dealt with the news and reality that the distance and time had not allowed him to see her those last five years, and that his only connection to his childhood was gone.

Then came another hurdle. The mortgage on our little house was due for renewal. The mortgager wanted to add, or have a bonus, of

$2000 before renewing the mortgage. That would have wiped out all the payments we had made to the principle of the mortgage over the last five years, not to mention that we did not have $2000! We did not consent, and moved into a rented two bedroom apartment that was actually half of an old stone farmhouse. Although we stayed there only one year it was an eventful year. That farmhouse had no indoor plumbing and after we were there for a few months the landlord decided to put a bathroom upstairs on our side, eliminating one of the two bedrooms. Irene had to sleep in Rainer's bedroom which was tactfully divided with a curtain. This would not do! It only added to the already cramped life in that apartment, as Joe and I slept in the living room. When the lease was up we moved to another rented house. This time it was a bigger three bedroom house; but after another year of renting, we decided it was time to save for a nominal down payment and buy. By the way, the old farm house is still standing, right there on King Street beside all the newer ones. We were glad to leave that farmhouse apartment, but not before we acquired another pet. When I look back today, I think it was our pets that helped relieve life's stress, and I am grateful for these creatures.

The family sharing this farm house, living in the apartment next to us, had a small mixed Spaniel. This beautiful long-haired dog was being abused by the family and their kids, and it was Irene who somehow managed to convince them to give it to her. This dog be- came one of my favorite pets, but it was almost three weeks before I even knew what its eyes were like. For many days it was shaking and cowering in a corner, and came out only to eat and do its business. This poor dog would shiver as soon as anyone approached her. It took a long while before our new dog, Sandy, became used to us, and then she turned into an affectionate, loveable dog. She lived with us for several years, and her personality developed to become a delight. She must have had something of a Scottish Shepherd in her for she was forever protecting anything that moved.

We went smelt fishing on the shore of Lake Ontario. We could not be fast enough to pick the smelts out of the net. Sandy would lie in front of the net growling and barring her teeth, snapping at us if we tried to remove the flip-flopping tiny fish. Then once, when we took a camping vacation, the boys from a neighboring tent were collecting bull frogs. These were huge frogs, bigger than a four month old kitten! When the boys came to show us the box of frogs, Sandy lay down beside the box intent on protecting them. Then something amazing happened. If I hadn't seen it with my own eyes, I would not have believed it. One of the frogs jumped out and went to the lake. Sandy followed. With several swift strokes the frog was well off shore, but then it stopped. The frog waited for Sandy to catch up, and then the two of them swam side-by-side for quite a while before Sandy returned to shore.

Months later, when the children acquired two small turtles, Sandy was again fascinated by them, and was very agitated when anyone touched the aquarium. At one time when Joe was doing some electrical work at a friend's farmhouse, he took Sandy with him for a run in the country. It was already evening when we were preparing to leave. We were standing by the car when a mouse ran across the yard. Sandy bounded after the mouse. The little animal stopped and then crawled into Sandy's fur. Only when we picked Sandy up did the mouse run away. But the most astonishing thing happened when years later, living in the country, we found a ground hog with an injured paw. We nursed it to health in a box behind our home. One day the paw was healed, the box was empty and ground hog gone. That same day we observed Sandy running in tight circles around something. On closer look it was the ground hog that Sandy was rounding up to move back to its box where Sandy thought it belonged.

Tragically, after nearly seven years with us she suddenly ran in front of a car and was fatally injured. The vet told me that she was already a very old dog and that this swift death was a blessing for her. We had other dogs in later years, but Sandy was never forgotten.

After working for five years with the lawyer in Whitby, he was appointed to a judge's position, and I found a job in Oshawa with another law firm, happy not to have to commute that long distance anymore. My son Rainer, many years later happened, quite by accident, to purchase the house that the Whitby lawyer, now a judge had lived in. It is a beautiful large bungalow on a magnificent ravine lot, and it was where Rainer and his wife raised their family.

I was knowledgeable in the legal procedures, and started work at the new firm with a substantial salary raise. Our lives now moved with a certain routine. Rainer finished high school and after completing the first year of university found work with a steel company for the summer. Lasco Steel offered him a job within his field, and the pay was so lucrative that Rainer continued his education while work- ing. He built his career, and stayed with the company until his retirement decades later.

Irene, the youngest, was still in high school when Joe and I be- came restless with the routine of day-to-day life. Although Joe kept his job, now with General Motors, I quit working as a legal secretary, and when a small restaurant, run by German acquaintances of ours, came up for sale, we bought it. The owner was terminally ill with cancer, but on his good days he would come and sit at the restaurant and help, introducing us to the many regular customers. The restaurant was located out of town on a busy highway leading to Peterborough (Highway 115). There was a sit-down dining room area and a lunch bar counter with stools, and the two areas were separated by a glass- enclosed gift counter.

With the restaurant we inherited a large dog of German Sheppard mix. During the day she was on a chain, but at night she was loose and patrolled the yard around the restaurant, never leaving the area. The previous owner told us that she was a good watch dog, and he never worried if he happened to forget to lock the door. One night a police car stopped on his route and one of the officers got out to see if everything was all right. *So,* the dog, (*So* was her name) did not bark but silently went up to the officer and bit him on the leg, leaving teeth marks right through his heavy trousers. He knocked at the door to report the incident, but without complaint, as he simply stated that *So* was doing her job.

The commute and the hectic pace became too much for Rainer as he was now working shifts at Lasco. It was time for him to move closer to work. He had already had a near disaster that became a clear warning to him. Right at our restaurant entrance to the high- way, in the early morning, the quiet was punctuated by the loud screeching of tires and the sickening noise of crunching cars. It was only seconds before that Rainer had left for work. This accident caused tremendous damage to his beloved Volkswagen but luckily for him, he escaped with just knee damage. He was doing a lot of travel- ing at this time in his life as he was now in a serious relationship. His girlfriend, who later became his wife and lifetime partner, was the daughter of a Dutch immigrant's family who had settled in another nearby town of Ajax. With courtship on his mind and the responsibilities of work, he moved and began a life of his own.

During the first few months at the restaurant, Irene, sixteen years of age, was allowed to drive the old car and continue with her high school in Oshawa. However, it was agreed that she would pick up pies for the restaurant at a bakery, especially on the days when Joe worked the night-shift and could not get them himself. I had never learned to bake a Canadian pie but homemade pies were very much asked for. Usually the pies were laid out in a big box for transport, but the baker did not always have enough boxes for all the pies. One day Irene arrived with quite a few pies that were not much good for anything but crumbs. The pies started out neatly lined up on the back seat, but after several sharp turns, many pies ended up between the seat and the passenger door!

Joe kept his job at General Motors until we could be sure that the restaurant was the right thing for us. He helped out in his spare time and after work with all the restaurant building maintenance, and there was much of that. I remember the day the toilet was plugged. It was the end of a long weekend and the restaurant was full. Upon reading the Closed For Repair sign on the ladies toilet, a mother with her young daughter of about six came to Joe stating that she urgently needed the toilet. Joe directed them to the men's restroom, which was right beside the ladies' restroom. He kept working with the plunger and all his plumbing tools and expertise, but nothing would un- block the stubborn clog. Then suddenly with a gush followed by a loud scream … from the little girl in the toilet next door, all was clear, but the girl needed a wash, and Joe full of apologies and embarrassment, was forgiven by the understanding mother.

Our restaurant was a great learning experience for all of us including Irene's boyfriend, Bob, who a few years later became her husband. He would often come to help, and was a great dishwasher and hamburger maker. By that time Joe and I already had our second boat, a small outboard cruiser, that Joe was constantly working on with what little spare time he had. One Sunday morning when it seemed clear that the slow business of the day before would be repeated, we decided to leave Irene and Bob in charge and take the day off. The day was sunny and relaxing and after supper on the boat we returned to the restaurant to find a closed sign on the door and sheer disaster inside. The dishwasher going full out with every dish dirty, the kitchen empty of home fries, no 'soup of the day' left and Irene and Bob excited but thoroughly exhausted. We realized that they had had a full day with more customers than I had envisioned. The full impact didn't hit me until I counted the till, and realized that in that one day they had made more than we had during the whole previous week! The reason for this onslaught of customers became clear a few days later when a regular customer explained that we had a wonderful write-up in the Toronto Star newspaper's restaurant section. It said to be sure and stop by because the home-cooked food was excellent and the daily German specials delicious. Irene explained that she had to ask for help at one point during the day.

There was a hydro crew working on a three-month contract in the area and they were daily supper regulars. When they came in for a Sunday meal, Irene asked one of them if he would help peel potatoes in exchange for a free supper. The poor fellow was too shy to refuse and much to the glee of his comrades, he helped.

As the months wore on we realized that we could use more help. When we bought the place there were a couple of waitresses and at first there was an older man, a part-time fellow who stayed on for a while. But he enjoyed his drink and could not be relied on. Being in the country on a highway, help was difficult to get. Then one day a customer over a coffee said he was a cook and would be happy to work here, but he would have to be able to board here as well, because he had no car. He was a good-looking man in his early forties, clean and dressed in a neat but worn suit. We agreed on a salary and allowed him to live in the small unfinished two-room bungalow that the previous owner had built on the property behind the restaurant. We found it peculiar that he arrived with just two paper bags of belongings. But he said he had been a cook in the military, and we needed the help. One summer day in the terrible heat of the kitchen I suggested that he remove his suit jacket. At first he hesitated but then revealed that he did not have a second shirt, and the one he wore had a huge tear in the back. Realizing that the two paper bags could not have carried much, I gave him clothes and other necessities that no longer fit my son, things he had left behind when he moved on.

Our life at the restaurant was busy, but not without some hilarious incidents. Very early one morning, as I opened the restaurant, I noticed that the large commercial dishwasher was running. I could not understand it, as we always left the restaurant clean with all the dishes washed when we closed up at eleven o'clock at night. It was seven am in the morning, and we have not yet had any customers! When the dishwasher stopped I opened it up to find, there all alone in the middle of the huge dish tray, the cook's dentures! While this cook was with us, he lived in the little partially-finished house behind the restaurant, and was allowed to use the furniture we were storing there, including our Hi Fi stereo. The cook loved classical music, and played it loud and often.

A customer who could not pay his rather large bill left us with a small quarter horse. He insisted that this was the only way he could settle his account (which by the way, we inherited when we bought the place). We appropriately named her Penny, but where on earth were we going to keep it? Although there was a small field of about half an acre around the little house behind the restaurant, there was no shed or barn. We made her a small enclosure with bales of hay, but her persistent whinnying indicated that she did not like it. There was an unfinished room attached to the house that was eventually supposed to be a garage. That is where we put Penny. For a while she was content, but the cook complained. There was a sliding door from this garage to the living room and every time the cook played his music, Penny would push the sliders open and stand there, head in the living room seemingly enjoying the classics.

We were not aware that Penny was pregnant when we got her and as time went on she became restless. We knew all along that we could not keep her, but to have a foal as well was out of the question. So Joe talked to a nearby farmer who had lots of land, and the same day that he picked her up, Penny gave birth to a beautiful foal. Penny, who was docile by nature, and the rusty-brown colored foal soon became a beloved addition for the farmer and his family, and we were completely satisfied that Penny had found the right home at last.

We soon found out that our cook was a very innovative cook; as well as making the daily German specials, there were other dishes he would make. During the winter months the specials were usually hearty stews and goulash. I remember sending him down to the basement for garlic and onion bulbs as they added taste to the soups and stews. But it wasn't till Spring, when I was looking for my dahlia flower bulbs that I realized he had used them too!

Then one day, just as quickly as this cook had appeared, he was gone. He took what he felt he was owed for that week's wages, left a note in the till and disappeared. We saw him once more when we came across him quite by accident. He seemed well, and told us that he never stayed anywhere longer than a few months!

Joe traveled a lot between the restaurant, work at General Motors, the baker in Whitby and the many other errands he had to run. He was always in a hurry because he knew his help was needed at the restaurant. After the fifth speeding ticket the police were ready to do more than just advise him to 'slow down if he valued his life'. The restaurant was starting to take its toll.

I practically ran the restaurant single handed — the cooking, the purchasing (of supplies and replenishing the gift shop area), cleaning, bookkeeping and so on. Located on the highway, the customers were sure to come, but help was difficult to get and the help we did have, we soon found was not too honest. They helped themselves to cigarettes, and when their friends came in, forgot to bill them. Even the often hilarious incidents did not make running the restaurant any easier.

We did meet some great folks though. For instance, there were the "Christmas tree millionaires", Americans who owned large Christmas tree plantations in our area. All through the summer, when tree pruning was going on and later in October and November when the trees were harvested, baled and ready for shipment to the US, these fellows would come very late every evening looking for supper. They were often exhausted and instead of choosing a meal they just said, "give us something nice to eat". I made sure that they had a different meal each time and later topped it off with a "German milk-shake" beer served in the large aluminum milk-shake mixing tumblers. A very much appreciated, if forbidden, gesture on my part.

The restaurant was open seven days a week, seven AM until eleven PM. A pretty hectic schedule, and even more so when summer traffic came. We were on the highway used by all the city dwellers heading out to cottages and the car-race enthusiasts heading out to the famous Mosport Race Track nearby. Joe and I by this time had acquired a small lot on Scugog Lake to go with our boat, and were attempting to clear the lot of trees. When I look back now it was as if we wanted to live our life all at once. Maybe this attitude was another legacy of the years lost during the war and its aftermath.

Pretty soon we found out that the restaurant ate too deeply into our time and energy. Even the satisfaction of being written up favor- ably in the Toronto newspaper and all the entertainment that the folks, customers and employees alike, provided could not make up for the total loss of private life. So after barely a year we put it up for sale. It took a while, but we finally sold it, and Joe, Irene and I, along with our dog Sandy , moved back to Oshawa.

The small pink-stoned, flat-roofed house on Chadburn street became a quiet haven after the hustle and bustle of the restaurant episode. I was glad that Joe had kept his job at General Motors as we realized that entrepreneurial restaurant management was not the way to improve our lot here in Canada. The house became even quiet- er when, a year later, Irene who had finished school, found a job at a bank in the city of Toronto and moved out. Although I had no difficulty finding work again with a legal firm, with my children grown and moved away, I had time to reflect. Life here had often been hectic and demanding, and many times my patience was worn thin, but immigrating into Canada had been a good thing and would provide better opportunities for my family and their future.

Now it was time to look ahead and enjoy our little house and garden as "empty nesters".

SIX

1970 - 2005

An empty nest; a full l i f e

Our beloved dog Sandy died while I was walking her in the neighborhood near that little pink house. We mourned for her, felt the loneliness of the children's absence, and with the excitement of the restaurant life over the house felt truly quiet. Then six months later, in mid August, Joe brought home a seven-week-old puppy. We named her Gussie. I was apprehensive at first. We really didn't need all the work of training a young dog! We were at work all day, and Gussie didn't understand outside business and of course she couldn't hold it that long. But Joe persisted, and finally we had a delightful pet that stayed with us for sixteen years. Gussie had the coloring of a Weimeraner and the small body of a terrier.

After the hectic time at the restaurant, those twelve years spent at this little pink house were wonderful. The grandchildren came to visit. The eldest, my daughter's girls, were able to spend the night at Oma's, and we had wonderful talks. I have memories of Irene's young toddlers playing with the water hoses in the back yard. Later Rainer's daughter, as a toddler, entertained us playing with Gussie. Although Gussie was a gentle dog, she would not share her toys, and as soon as she heard the child at the front door, that dog rushed about gathering up all her toys, stuffing them into her box. The little child was quick and figured out that there was more in that box than just the dog and often pulled the toys out right from under the dog.

Now that Joe and I were alone, we traveled a lot and we took our small dog with us. In summer you would find us on our boat. All his life Joe loved boats and water. We were now fortunate to have purchased a larger used cabin-cruiser that he repaired, and which served us well as we traveled the many waterways of Ontario. We boated up through the Trent Canal system, marvelling at the engineering of the many locks, especially the world-famous hydraulic lift locks in Peter- borough. We traveled through many lakes from Lake Scugog, Balsom Lake and Lake Simcoe, and traveled right up to the open waters of Georgian Bay. It was on one of these trips that we encountered one of the sudden storms that Lake Simcoe is famous for.

When we set out from the shore, the weather was beautiful and the lake calm. Lake Simcoe is a relatively shallow lake, and terrible storms can spring up without warning, bringing on turbulent waves that are a challenge to even the skilled sport boater. We were just past the mid-point when the weather became steadily worse. I still cringe as I remember how we almost floundered. Waterlogged and exhausted after what seemed like hours, we were able to drag the cruiser to the safety of a small inland channel where we waited out the squall, which stopped almost as quickly as it had started. Nervously we busied ourselves bailing out the boat, trying not to think of what could have happened.

Soon all was forgotten and the open waters of Georgian Bay beckoned us. We exchanged the cruiser for a larger boat. The cruiser was sold to a retired couple who wished to enjoy the boating life that they so admired. However as they had never operated a boat, Joe agreed to spend a weekend with them showing them the 'ropes'. Later he was to be plagued with feelings of guilt, and wished he had insisted that they take professional lessons that are offered at the various marinas. After enjoying only a few weekends on their new boat, tragedy struck. While still tied to the dock, they were enjoying drinks with friends, showing off their boat, when the husband accidentally hit the ignition and his wife, who was sitting on the rail, fell over- board. The boat lunged back and she was fatally crushed between the boat and the dock.

We kept our larger boat for a couple of summers, but Joe's enjoyment of motor boating had waned. We sold the cruiser and opted for a sail boat, a small one at first, then later, we managed to acquire a Buccaneer yacht which slept eight people, and was completely equipped and ocean worthy. Although it was expensive, we manipulated our finances, and the equity in our beautiful little pink house provided a new mortgage to purchase this yacht. I wasn't too keen on these finances, however, this fine yacht became the envy of many a yachtsman and fulfilled a life time dream for Joe. Later, after this sailboat was transported by means of a huge transport truck from Toronto to Georgian Bay, and once we were on the open water, all my stress seemed to float away as I too enjoyed the yacht.

Our friend and neighbor, who owned the lot next to ours on the Scugog River, was as eager to buy that larger 2nd cruiser as Joe was eager to go sailing. Joe felt a little more secure selling it to him but that too proved misguided. Although this time there was no tragedy, the cruiser did sink, slowly, overnight. One weekend the new owner left the drain plug open while the boat was docked only to return the next weekend to see the cabin roof barely above water!

Sailing on Georgian Bay, Beausoleil Island was our frequent destination. The vast expanse of water with the many islands holds a warm and special memory for me. We would often dock in one of the secluded bays and then enjoy Beausoleil Island, itself with its own little lake, many paths and walkways. In the early years we put up a tent but later we simply slept on our sail boat, and allowed the rocking motion to take life's stress away. Life again had a routine, although still a busy one. The weekdays were spent at work, then caring for our house and all the chores involved with that; but by Thursday evening I made sure that the bags were once again packed with freshly laundered weekend clothes, food pre-cooked and packed so that on Friday when Joe picked me up from work, we never had to go back to our home, and instead headed straight to the Bay. There were times when I wondered if the hectic pace of the week was worth it. But once I woke up Saturday morning to the lapping sound of water splashing against our boat, I was quite content with the inconveniences of camping and boating, and I looked forward to spending time catching up on my reading. One lucky summer we were even able to take time from work and spend three weeks on the boat!

After the restaurant, when I was working once again at a law office, I found I had time to finally pursue my life-long dream, and I enrolled in a correspondence course for journalism with the News-paper Institute of America. It was a challenge. Although I had limited time available to devote to this passion, I completed the course in three years. It was worthwhile and rewarding. With 98% on my final exam, I was proud, as I thought my German accent didn't show in the written word!

It was during these years that my interest in many varied topics took hold. My readings and personal studies included ancient history, mythology, religions of the world and of course all current events. I found astronomy fascinating, and I learned the old art of astrology and numerology, and studied ancient Egyptian myths and Old Testament philosophy. For fun I prepared natal charts for those in the family who were interested. These were not just "pie in the sky" predictions, but charts driven by the numbers calculated with date of birth, including exact time, place of birth, with longitude and latitude. Then the calculations had to be precise with the astrological configurations of that time. I could not do these huge calculations alone, and much studying was involved as computers had not yet become available.

I also volunteered to teach German on Saturdays to children at the German Club here in Oshawa. We were busy. Still full time at work, but with summer holidays and weekends spent on the lakes in Ontario; winter holidays were spent in Florida! Joe didn't like the cold and was eager to escape to the tropical climate as soon as General Motors closed for the Christmas holidays. For twelve years we packed up the car, took the dog and drove that long trek south so we could spend three weeks in the sun! We missed Christmas with our adult children, and grandchildren, but often, in lieu of the holidays, we spent time with them before we left. Our dog, Gussie, enjoyed travel too as she slept in motels on her own comforter that we brought for her. Each year we went to a different destination, from St. Augustine to the Everglades. We basked in the lush tropical gardens, not to mention the terrific beaches.

Our many trips south made Joe lust for the warmer climate even more. So I was not surprised at what happened in New Smyrna Beach, near Daytona. I pointed to a small motel with a lavish garden and flowering bushes in front. On these trips we had a routine. We always looked for a motel, then Joe went into make sure that we would be welcome with our dog. This motel, although it had a large front yard, was a relatively small place with 10 guest rooms. Joe went inside while I waited. It took what seemed like an endless amount of time, and I was just about to go look for him when he appeared with the owner who showed us to our room. By the look on their faces I knew something was up. Sure enough, Joe asked me if I wanted to own this place as it was up for sale!

Within a very short time an offer was made and accepted. Joe had visions of sunny retirement years in a warm climate, with income from the motel to supplement his pension. We came back to Canada, and now we had to sell our little pink house, the beautiful yacht, and once again I had to leave my legal secretarial job. We had the remain- der of the winter, all of spring and by the end of June it was done. Now for the first time we were driving to Florida in the middle of the hot summer instead of during the Christmas holidays. And we were pulling a trailer full of the belongings that were left after our sale with the few things that we wanted to take with us on our journey to "our Motel". Thus began a year that I can only call "another adventure"!

Again, as with the restaurant, the owners stayed with us to show us the ropes and clear up the rest of the paperwork involved with ownership transfer. All too soon I was on my own again for Joe had to return to work in Canada. He had been many years with General Motors, but still did not have enough working time accumulated to retire on. Besides we wanted to make absolutely sure that the motel move was the right one and that it would work for us. Surely after running a restaurant, with all the hassles of cooking, staffing and all, and during the busy part of our life when we still had two teenaged children at home, renting out rooms should seem like a piece of cake!

Joe was off but would come back very soon as he would try to get as much time off from General Motors as possible, not just on the Christmas Holidays. Sometimes he came down for a few weeks but mostly I plunged, at full speed, into the business of running a motel by myself. The previous owner had introduced me to a lady who would come to work for me, so I had a helper. But I soon realized that this was not enough, and I managed to arrange a laundry service to rotate the linens. I made sure that along with laundering the bedding and towels, the small carpets at the foot of the bed were also laundered regularly. Anything to help reduce the workload.

This year would become an overwhelming experience. I was alone, too busy to realize how much I missed my family, and once again caught in a hectic work schedule. Drinking began to soothe my nerves.

My eyes were opened further as my lessons in life continued. The lush gardens of the winter months in Florida faded as the heat of the summer changed the garden climate, and the people that passed through my motel life were varied and challenging to say the least.

There was the couple who told me a story that they worked in the bar next door, and were having their house trailer repaired. Would I mind if they brought their toddler and some belongings with them while they stayed at the motel. I wanted to be helpful and said ok, thinking that they must be working opposite shifts to look after their youngster. But the next morning I noticed another young woman, who had obviously slept there, come out of the room and then still another young man. I asked the woman what were they thinking having four persons and a toddler staying in the room. I was told it was the boyfriend of the babysitter. That was too much and I asked them to leave immediately.

Another morning I awoke to find two men sitting in my front garden, shading themselves under the table's umbrella, enjoying sandwiches and beer. Beside them was a tent that they had set up. When I asked them why didn't they ring the night bell, that I would have gladly rented them a room, the answer came bluntly that "they wanted to spare themselves the expense and were just having breakfast now". When I questioned the police about what I could do about this situation, the police replied "Nothing, if they don't litter or leave a mess there is nothing wrong with pitching a tent on private property!" Florida — new laws to understand!

Almost every day there was some irregularity in that business. Once an elegantly dressed gentleman wanted to rent the room closest to the curl in the far end of the driveway. I had a nervous feeling about it, and quoted him an exorbitant price hoping to scare him away. It didn't work. He accepted the high price and paid without batting a eye. Then soon large dark expensive cars came. The drivers would drive up, go to this man's room, and after a few minutes come out and drive away. This went on for the entire night. He checked out the next morning without ever having slept in his bed. Later I was to find out that he was involved in the drug business, and was obviously collecting money from his runners. Luckily I never saw him or the drivers of the expensive cars again!

New Smyrna, where the motel was, is close to Daytona, famous for its car-racing track. I had race drivers and mechanics with all their equipment spend time here. In peak racing season with motel rooms unavailable anywhere in Daytona, I often had to do some creative re-arranging as I did not want to lose business. It goes with- out saying that I was always glad when my family came to visit, but, putting them up was always a challenge, especially when they came during the peak tourist season! We had two private bedrooms with our living quarters attached to the motel. Often the family doubled up in those bedrooms. Once I even had to put a customer, one that I knew was completely trustworthy, in that second bedroom. My daughter Irene and her two young children found their way down by hitching a ride with a co-worker who came for the races. My son and his young family came during the winter tourist season and at the same time my sister, Frieda, her daughter, Ingrid with her husband, Heinze, came all the way from Berlin, Germany. My daughter Monika, who was convalescing with a broken leg, accompanied Joe on one of his many trips down that year. On another occasion Joe brought two elderly friends with him from Oshawa, Canada. As Joe was always looking to have company on that long drive down, and that often meant non-paying guests who had to be looked after, beds had to be found, time had to be stretched … and all that during the peak season! I was glad, yet totally exhausted.

My family wanted to see Florida. The grandchildren were excited about Disney World and all the other attractions there, but often I could not accompany them, with business first. But there were times, when Joe was there, when we simply put up a no-vacancy sign, and went on our way.

I developed a plan to rent rooms to construction crews that worked in the area. That way I could get references and was assured that clients stayed longer that just a night or two. I also made sure that folks who lived in the area did not rent one of my rooms. I wanted no more 'business' conducted from the rooms, and often found myself simply reasoning with them that they should go home. Slowly I felt some semblance of control, although banking and other Florida institutions were still difficult and sometimes puzzling. Often I was paid in cash but because it was late at night, and the banks here had very specific hours for commercial banking, I had to find a safe way to store the money until the next banking day. Our dog, Gussie, was my assistant. She didn't like strangers, and bared her teeth menacingly if any one came too close. So I put the cash under her bed cushion.

Not only was the police enforcement and some of the laws hard to understand, I was also saddened by the health care system here. Al- though I was well taken care of, many of the elderly Floridians simply didn't seek medical help as it was just too expensive. A broken finger or gash would just have to heal on its own.

Winter holidays in Florida are great. The weather is warm and temperate, the flowers are in full bloom, and a special cleaning is done on all the streets before the arrival of tourists. But to work here, in the off season, is another story. The weather is hot and humid, and the flowers are replaced by dry cactus and palmetto bugs, a lovely Florida name for cockroaches. Although exciting, a tropical storm, with its sudden downpour of torrential rain can be devastating to property and plants alike. I missed the changing of the seasons. In Florida they were hardly noticeable. There was simply a warm tourist season and the hot sticky summer with the locals and teenagers just hanging around.

Once a reporter and her photographer wanted to make reservations for the Daytona races. They insisted on staying here because they had heard that this motel was "clean" with no prostitutes or people who wanted a room for one night even though they lived in the area. That made me feel good, and my efforts to keep this motel respectable had paid off.

Joe made every attempt to come down. There was always work to be done that I could not do or had difficulty hiring out. Once when our water system seemed sluggish he went to investigate. The well on our property was overrun with vegetation, so he promptly stretched out on the ground, rolled up his sleeve and put his hand down to pull out the weeds. Neighbors quickly came to stop him. There could be poisonous snakes or even alligators they shouted, after all we were in the tropics! Alligators? Once a neighbor friend complained that he had to get one out of his swimming pool.

To free up more time from his job at General Motors, Joe scheduled a knee operation. Previously he felt he could have lived without the surgery, and endured the pain associated with his knee, but now he figured the time off could be spent here with me. Several times he had driven straight through from Ontario to Florida, stopping only for a brief rest at the roadside. Often, during that year, he only had a week off and couldn't afford the time on the road. But this time, with the knee just out of surgery, I was really worried, and tremendously relieved when he arrived.

We talked. The work, the climate of 92 F with 92% humidity, the distance from the family all affected us. We resolved that we were better off with our world in Oshawa and work with General

Motors. The dream of an easy retirement was not quite what we thought it was supposed to be. We sold the motel. A couple from Quebec with the same dream but with more experience, as they had a similar business in Canada, expressed interest. We made the deal lucrative for them by offering to hold a second mortgage thus they could take over almost immediately. Soon we were again on our way back to Canada, driving the distance together while towing our overstuffed trailer with our personal possessions behind.

We planned the border crossing into Canada carefully so that we would arrive after midnight. We had visions of the border guards inspecting and removing our belongings from the trailer. We wanted to make sure that there was minimal traffic at the border to make their job easier, and mostly to avoid the embarrassment of seeing our meagre belongings stretched out in front of us. Our worries were unfounded as the crossing was uneventful, and we made it to the outskirts of Oshawa, before the axel on the trailer gave out. Inching our way to a friend's house, we left the fully-loaded trailer there, where it stayed for the rest of the summer. Joe had rented a cottage on Buckhorn Lake while he looked for a house to buy in Oshawa.

Here at this lake-side cottage with the open Canadian landscape, and the peace of the countryside, I was able to breathe and heal. Only the occasional trip to Oshawa and the trailer to retrieve some personal items and clothes interrupted the stillness. On these trips I gradually rekindled my life.

It was only one hectic year in Florida, but I had missed more than the seasons and family. I missed my involvement with the Toast Mistress Club. (Now called ITC , International Training in Communication.) Some years ago, back when we were living in that lovely pink flat-roofed house in Oshawa my sister, Christa, had introduced me to this club and I was immediately fascinated. I was trained to give all sorts of speeches, do book reviews, and in parliamentary procedures. The pledge when I was installed was "I hereby pledge to give active thought to leadership training and speech improvement, hoping through better communication to achieve greater understanding throughout the world". And the motto was "To use our language with grace and facility". The theme was service and truth — I had come full circle.

After we sold the motel and immediately upon returning to Oshawa, I rejoined the Oshawa Club. Sure there had been clubs in Florida, but I had had no time or energy to participate.

I continued with the ITC for nearly 28 years, even after we eventually moved from Oshawa yet again. During my time with the club I learned a great deal, and even achieved the Third level in Parliamentary procedure according to "Roberts' Rule of Order". I won several speech contests and worked in almost every level of the organization. Six or seven local clubs made up a Council and several Councils made a Region. Our Oshawa Club, was of the Great Lakes Region, and also was made up of Southern Ontario, Michigan, Ohio and Kentucky, a truly international organization with headquarters in Anaheim, California. My work with them, at the different levels, provided me the opportunity to travel to a great many of the functions and geographical locations. Through my 28-year involvement with the club, I became President of our chapter and held that post, off and on, for 10 years.

Upon our arrival back from the Motel adventure, and before we could really settle in Oshawa, I stayed for the summer at that rented cottage on Buckhorn Lake, with our belongings stored at a friend's place. Although Joe remained during the week in his rented room in Oshawa while continuing his work at General Motors, he would spend weekends with me at Buckhorn. I rested peacefully at the lake, enjoy- ing the company of my eldest granddaughter, who came visiting often. Since Joe and I didn't have much time to settle back in Oshawa, somehow it made sense to build a home in the country, instead of buying. We began building a prefab Viceroy home on our lot in Sugar- bush on Pigeon Lake. Joe continued to commute weekly to Oshawa to work and I commuted to the ITC when I could, and on weekends and holidays we were builders!

Thus began a very rewarding adventure. There were so many arrangements to be made, the excavating for a basement, drilling of a well, aligning a plumber and other tradesmen. We did a lot of the work ourselves and as soon as the house was reasonably liveable, I moved in. The years I lived in that Sugarbush house with Joe coming on weekends was a refreshing and enjoyable time. I had time and a place for my grandchildren to come during the summer. Irene's children, now in grades four and five, enjoyed nature and the great out- doors while spending some of their summer holidays with me.

At my eldest granddaughter's wedding, my guests from Germany, my sister Carin and her husband Ziggi enjoyed the great Canadian outdoors and scenery at Sugarbush. The daily walks with my dog when we went through the woods to the lake and the absolute freedom were wonderful. I was able to catch up on my reading and thoughts, and with all that fresh air, my health improved.

But in time it became clear to me that it was impossible for Joe to make the regular trips back and forth to Oshawa to work, and the weekend was not enough time together. With a heavy heart we put the Sugarbush house up for sale.

After much thinking Joe decided that since he was so close to retirement, maybe, if we bought a small three-storey apartment house with three small units in it, we could live in one and supplement our income making our retirement a bit better.

Now I was a landlady! Worst of all, the location of this apartment house was very close to the highway intersection that was used mainly by G. M. traffic as workers commuted right past our house to- and-from work. And the bus depot was also located at the end of this intersection. Every bus in the city made at least two trips past our house! The traffic, the noise! It was so bad that the windows shook, and the radio and television volume had to be turned full volume to be heard. I requested the property tax assessor to come, but once here he could not hear me unless I shouted. The taxes were reduced by 20%. But I was definitely not happy.

The closer Joe came to his retirement year, the more he talked about buying another lot and building again, maybe this time closer to the city. At work one of Joe's friends, who lived in Warkworth, a small village about three quarters of an hour out of town, told him to check this place out. Here, he said, you could buy a house fairly cheap, almost for the same price that a vacant city lot would have cost.

I had never heard of Warkworth and to say I was apprehensive again is an understatement! I found it on a local map. It was a tiny dot in the middle of nowhere. I told Joe I would agree to move into a country home only if there was a doctor, pharmacy, bank, post office, food store, and all had to be within walking distance of the house! I was balking and this time I wanted to be firm.

But Joe convinced me to come with him, at least for a ride to see the village. Lets just consider it an outing, he said. OK, I agreed and off we went for a car ride and coffee. As soon as we left the main highway I began to enjoy the drive over the rolling countryside, through the wooded area and the hills that surrounded Warkworth. With seven hills around the village and every road leading into the valley where this little village was, a different and more beautiful view awaited us. All the facilities I mentioned were there on Main Street, and we stopped and ate at a small village café and talked with the friendly owner, who as it happens, was also German. We learned a lot from her, and the information brought the village to life for us. There were close to five hundred people living there, and it was a center for the surrounding farmers, as the big Co-Op and Feed store indicated. I was sold on the idea of yet another move.

Shortly afterwards we found a house suitable to our budget and Joe's plans. It was at the foot of a hill with an acre lot. There was a paved road on each side with farmland surrounding it, but we were still only two blocks from Main Street. We knew that this old farm house, which had been empty for many years, would require a lot of repairs, but it was Joe's answer to his big question of what to do when he retired. Once we took possession we put up mouse traps and of course the dog, Gussie chased away what she could, but she was getting quite old. The farm house had some history and was built in 1882. We even found an old photo that showed the house with the now long-gone veranda, where the owners posed in turn-of-the-century clothes.

The house still boasted many of its original features and a charm that showed through the much-needed repairs. There were high ceilings, huge baseboards, a summer kitchen, a beautiful staircase with oak railing and even an old French door. The repairs were a bit overwhelming. However, Joe insisted that all could be done, and the house was solid. So once again we packed, sold our apartment house and prepared to move again.

We took possession of the Warkworth house on a cold day in March, 1982. The doors didn't close properly, the kitchen was in disarray. The outside wooden door was warped and let snow in. The kitchen was our first concern. The window over the sink was broken and had been repaired with newspaper, dated 1960. There was a small room next to the kitchen, which we called the summer kitchen, that led to the garage, and also to the basement where the stairs were broken and some of the basement fieldstones showed cracks. Joe said this was all no problem, and the basement walls were tremendously thick. Also, there in the basement was a huge square concrete cistern that was probably used to collect rain water in earlier days, but now was full of all sorts of garbage.

Although there was a modern oil furnace and even an old wood stove in the kitchen, the pipes leading to the chimney were exposed and running directly through the kitchen! That was the first thing we removed, but not until the stove served its purpose as a garbage incinerator. What a mess! The linoleum in the oversized kitchen was full of oil stains. We found out from a previous owner that the tenants had repaired a motorcycle in the kitchen. The summer kitchen had a huge hole in the floor, a great entrance for any animal looking for shelter in our house.

That first spring was another nightmare but, the house had to be made liveable and room-by-room Joe worked. Our funds were low, but our imagination, experience and the friends we made showed us the way. Although exhausting, for we were both in our late fifties, we looked forward and worked together, interrupted only by the wonderful visits as our kids and grandkids came to explore our new village surroundings.

While Joe was occupied with the house, I began to plan a garden. The first thing on my agenda was to plant some trees, a mountain ash and some poplars on the border between us and an empty lot next door. Later there was to be an apple tree, two cherry trees, a chestnut tree, two birches and a Russian olive tree.

We had many adventures in re-building. Joe moved the kitchen sink and changed the cupboards to a more convenient location. He also did work on the exterior and holes had to be drilled. The walls of the house were thick. Drilling took great effort, and on one occasion Joe became worried as the hole he was drilling from the outside, which was almost through to the kitchen, started to smoulder and smoke. Worried about a fire, he hastily grabbed the garden hose, stuck it into the hole and sprayed. I was on the other side of that hole peeling potatoes, shocked from my daydream as the cold wet spray came through the wall straight at my face.

Always inventive, and intent on using the materials at hand, Joe was delighted to find cans of paint in the basement. After installing a long shelf in the huge closet he had finished for the master bedroom, he decided to use up this paint to seal the wood. It took weeks for that lovely brown paint to dry, until he finally he realized that it wasn't paint at all but oil left over from the many oil changes for cars and machinery at that farm house. To solve the problem, he decided to cover the brown paint with a coat of varnish. We had the most beautiful glossy smooth shelf with the wood finished nice enough to be a lovely piece of furniture; too bad it was on the inside of the closet.

Our kids contributed with practical gifts, helping out when they visited, such as the huge ceiling fan for the living room and the trees for the garden which my son supplied along with other practical gifts; my daughter's beautiful butterfly ornaments, but the double extension ladder and step stool were extremely useful as this house was a taller than average two story farmhouse. My eleven year old grandson, enjoyed a week of his summer vacation with us, was always fascinated with fire, and Joe put him in charge of keeping the backyard garbage fire under control, leaving Joe running back and forth as he found more left-over wooden building materials to burn. After a deck was built and the front entrance steps repaired, the whole property began to have a lived-in look and became more inviting, allowing me to look forward to more relaxed visits with family and friends.

After one short but busy year at our Warkworth farm house, a cloud that could not be repaired fell over me. I was diagnosed with lung cancer. That diagnosis came barely eight weeks after my sister, Christa, who had also immigrated to Canada, had passed away with the same disease. I was devastated at the loss of my sister, and barely comprehending what was happening to me. I was lucky. With extreme urgency my doctor ordered a biopsy, and within a week I had major surgery to remove part of my lung. It took me a long time to recover but I continued free of the disease for many years. My grand- daughter gave birth to my first great-grand child during this time; as we were both in the hospital at the same time, I was saddened that I was too ill to fully enjoy this occasion.

I came home to convalesce, glad to be with Joe and my beloved dog Gussie, who by now was nearly 16 years old. Shortly afterwards, too old and ill, she had to be put down. I was getting more and more depressed and tired.

Joe, concerned and still busy with the house, thought another dog would be great company, but the thought of another dog to get attached to and look after, seemed overwhelming. Then after almost a year, I conceded and stated that if he could find a small, short- haired, female lap dog I might consider it. Joe told the local veterinarian that if he found such an animal that needing a home, we might adopt her. Almost the very next day the vet called, and when I asked if the dog was female, short-haired and small, he answered "Yes, it was only 25 pounds". When Joe came back from the vet's, I was shocked as the dog that walked into the kitchen was a large, black, long-haired cross between a lab and retriever. The only reason she weighed so little was because she was starved. Once again I was won over. As soon as I looked at her and the eagerness with which she ate a dish of food, then looked up at me with those sad brown eyes, I agreed that we'd keep her. After the initial shock, I began to like her. But she wasn't really my dog until some time later.

She thoroughly enjoyed the attention Joe lavished on her. She was brushed, played with, and while she was still light enough to be picked up, she even became a lap dog. That was quite a sight, Joe sitting on a kitchen chair with this huge dog draped over his lap, both quite content and happy. We named her Sonja, though it sound- ed like Sunny with our German accents, and it was because of her sunny disposition that we gave her this name.

For seven years we puttered, renovated and enjoyed that house. We had occasional trips and of course our boat trips continued, now one-day outings only. Although we had sold the huge sailing boat when we purchased our Motel in Florida, Joe always needed a boat and now we had a more manageable cruiser that he could tow quite easily to one of the many lakes that were within an hour drive of home. One of our favorite places to go boating and picnicking was a mere thirty-minutes drive away. Joe had retired in 1982 and we were relatively free to enjoy roaming, except for our ever-present pets. Sonja didn't like to ride in the car the way Gussie had. We reasoned that Sonja must have been taken by car and abandoned somewhere before she was rescued and taken to the vet. So we left her to watch the property, which she left only to accompany me on my walks to town. By now we also had a cat. My granddaughter moved from her country home in Buckhorn to an apartment in the city and could not take her cat. Zak, a rather huge orange tabby got along quite well with Sonja; that is to say they tolerated each other. But Sonja outdid the cat when it came to catching the many wild mice that tried to establish residence in our garage. Zak would let the mice go right by his nose, but Sonja, without breaking her stride, would squash any mouse that came too nearby simply stepping on it with her large paw. Once, when a mouse disappeared into a small gap in the foundation, Sonja sat there for hours waiting for the mouse to reappear. Then with one tap of her paw the mouse was gone and Sonja would walk on. When I went for my walks both animals would follow me over the hill behind our house, through an old abandoned apple orchard, sniffing and enjoying the freedom and yet still in my company. We were quite the trio en route to the village.

I mention my pets because my grandchildren were so enamored with them, and as they read these pages I hope it brings back wonderful childhood memories of visits with Oma and Opa and how much we enjoyed their visits and sharing our experiences.

Just before Joe retired he came home on one of his last days from work and said that he had a gift for me, and brought in a large wire cage with a rat in it. Not a cute little white rat like the ones Irene had brought home in her childhood but a larger, so-called white rat with brown spots on its rump; even his long tail was brown spotted. He explained that a colleague had asked him if he knew someone who would take care of it as he had grown tired of it and didn't want it any more; as it was tame, a pet, it would be a shame to let it die. Joe, the animal lover that he was, said that he would take it, but he would have to let his wife see it first. I named him Ringo, for his brown spots and rings. Ringo became a delightful entertainment especially for my youngest grandson who played with it often.

Ever the adventurers, Joe and I were always open to new experiences, and had a lot of entertainment with a (paid) hobby that we found to be fun. We applied and were both accepted as acting extras for movie sets that were filming in Toronto. This got us out on excursions other than boating. But we had to be prepared to be on the set all day and sometimes we were required to show up by dawn. We loved the excitement, first the training to get onto the casting lists, then registering with an agent and then the short parts. I remember the time Joe was called to be an extra on the TV series "Street Legal". We didn't do this for long, as the drive from Warkworth to Toronto was at least two hours, but 1987 was a great "acting" year.

Joe always kept busy with the house but when he decided to build a double garage, roof first, I was a bit concerned. He extended the roof line of the existing summer kitchen by supporting it with the traditional two-by-four framing. Then he closed in the walls, covered the exterior walls, and only then did he call in the cement mixer and had the contractor pour cement for the garage floor. I'm not sure if building a garage like this had ever been done before but the building inspector was called after the fact; he said that since it was completed, and was sturdy, with electrical codes passed, he would okay the whole thing. We were lucky!

Now Joe's beloved boat and the car had a home. That garage be- came a workshop, dog parlor and even an entertainment hall. In September 1989, my sister Carin and her husband once again visited Canada from Berlin, and we had a family gathering. What fun we had! The garage was decorated by the grandchildren and great- grandson. My nephew, Martin, who by now had children of his own, twin boys, was also there with his family and the boys got into decorating as well. It seemed that everyone was here, the kids, various spouses, girlfriends and boyfriends. Time and love had multi- plied our little family here in Canada, and we all remember that wonderful barbecue, for everything changed after that.

On January 13, 1990, Joe drove to service the car on a Saturday morning. He returned for lunch and after a hearty meal, went to visit friends to record a video. He came home in the late afternoon, and not feeling well said he would lie down for a short rest. He asked me for a glass of coke to help relieve his heartburn. By the time I came back with the drink, he had died of a massive heart attack.

I was in shock, as was the whole family. I had always been the one to get sick. Joe was active and healthy and only in his mid-sixties. It took me the better part of a year to come to terms with this, and my family was a great help.

Now I was alone with Sonja. For many days the dog waited at the end of the driveway for Joe to come home. But she soon became attach- ed to me, and with two animals to look after, I tried to keep busy.

Now the final repairs were my burden. The exterior of our huge two-story farm house was wood and although painted several years ago when Joe hired professionals to spray paint (a three-day job leaving much of the splatters on my flowers, shrubs and window ledges), the outside of the house was now shabby-looking again and a worry for me. The boat was also a concern. With much emotion and heavy work, the children and I moved the boat to the front lawn and put a For Sale sign on it. Even though I felt in control, life was a blur without Joe.

But life works in strange ways, and I felt blessed with the next event. A contractor who dealt in vinyl siding stopped by and looked at the boat. We struck a deal. The boat would be the down payment for refinishing the house, and a short-term, low-interest loan would pay for the rest. My house looked beautiful when it was finished and the crew even put siding on Sonja's little dog house to match.

All the major repairs to the house had been completed with one major exception: the water supply. The well was about three hundred feet from the house. It was very shallow, and seemed to always give trouble and run dry during the late summer. Joe and I had often thought that during these dry spells we should have the well filled, but no water truck could climb up the steep hill to the well. Our neighbors were great; we took two long garden water hoses, connect- ed to the neighbor's house, placed the hose through the empty lot next door, and let the water flow directly into our well. Their house was connected to city water but it was the last lot to be serviced on our street. After Joe died I convinced myself that I should have a new well drilled. They drilled and drilled, but the new well was a disappointment too. It was a couple of years later that the city extended the water pipes, so I too was on city water, but it was too late, for by now I had spent most of my savings.

I lived alone in that big house for seven years. My children came to visit me, and my brother-in-law, George, Christa's husband continued to be a regular monthly visitor. The dog and cat kept me comp- any, and thank God for the telephone! I traveled twice to Berlin and visited with my two sisters; I visited with Joe's cousin Lydia, and I went to several shows to hear my favorite tenor, Jose Carreras, sing. My son, Rainer, took me to see the "The Phantom of the Opera" and other concerts. I volunteered at the local public school to organize the library. But mostly I listened to my classical music at my kitchen window while I busied myself with needlework, and I read.

In time the house became too much for me and shortly after Sonja died at the ripe old age of 14, Irene convinced me to move closer to the family which was mostly in Oshawa, and get an apartment there. The large farm house had been renovated, decorated and repaired through the years, with the double garage and porch was wonderful, and all was surrounded by a huge garden, but too much to handle and too lonely. The decision to move was made easier as the new folks that purchased the farm house decided that they would keep the cat, Zak. Their young daughter had fallen in love with him.

It was pure luck that the right apartment was found almost the same day as the farm house had sold. I had often dreamed but never believed that such an apartment was possible for me. The view from this top floor was heavenly. I could still see all the beautiful trees that up until then, I was sure I would miss. The apartment was smack in the middle of Oshawa, convenient to all sorts of stores, pharmacies and so on. But its real beauty was the thirty-three meter long balcony, along the whole length of the apartment. As the apartment was empty, I rented it for one month prior to the final sale. Thus I had one whole month to clear up my belongings and decide what I would like to move with me. Irene was there, ready to work, box and sort, but on the final moving day, my son and his wife, and my granddaughter's husband Bob, were there as well and the move, although emotional, went smoothly.

For four years that apartment became my home. I missed the animals but it was nice to have family close by who could stop for coffee, rather than have them plan a day trip to Warkworth. I enjoyed my latest great-grandson, who was only a baby at this time. But best of all, I had more time to work on the typewriter, gathering my thoughts.

Then disaster struck. I had a stroke, and understood that living alone in the apartment was going to be too much. It was time to leave and go into a retirement home. While once again downsizing my belongings and getting me settled in the beautiful retirement home where I was to have a studio-bed-sitting room, Irene found the box with all the notes I had written through the years on my memoirs. Although we had talked and worked on these before, we now began to spend much time together, and for the next couple of years we spent many hours talking, as I recalled more memories and answered her many questions. The pages grew to become this book.

Every life has its challenges, and mine had its share. But I can reflect and be happy for a full life shared with Joe, grateful for his sense of adventure, humor and happy that his sense of duty and commitment carried us to Canada, where the children could spend their youth busy, safe, and look forward to their own future. Now I have time to let my mind wander, relive old memories and be thankful.

All and any of the information contained within this publication are presented with full written, witnessed permission for copyright with respect to the memoirs of Dorothea (Gutzeit) Koenigsberger by Dorothea Koenigsberger. Any information contained within this publication are the memories, opinions and references of Dorothea, thereby disclaiming any questionable, offensive or disputable issues that may arise and thereby absolve the author of any question- able, offensive or disputable issues. Documents pertaining to the family tree research and chronology are supported with various documents, including the *Ahnenpas* (record of ancestry), marriage and death certificates and other various documents.

I hereby give to my daughter Irene the right to file for the copyright in her name only to any book she might write based on the memoirs I have written about our family.

Dated at Whitby, Ont., this 9th day of May 2002.

Witness

Dorothea Koenigsberger

ANCESTORS' HISTORY

As I write about our ancestors, as much as I know of them, I imagine that we can think of ourselves as a train, and out of each window looks a different ancestor. We have inherited something from each, a certain disposition, trait or characteristic, even physical looks. I find the repetition of names amusing, especially since the ancestors' names were unknown to the new parents who named their offspring! It is with curiosity of the past that we find direction for the future, and I think it is important to know from whence we came, and thereby hope to find a better understanding of ourselves.

My childhood memories and the talks I had with various family members provided a lot of information. Birth, death and marriage certificates all aided in assimilating the data on my ancestors.

However the bulk of the data came from the *Ahnenpas*.

During my father's years, every German of position had to have an *Ahnenpas* to prove Aryan ancestry. During the 1920's and on, until the Second World War, the researching of ancestors became a thriving profession in Germany. My father had been a career soldier as a Cavalry Officer in the German Army during WWI and later held a civil service position with the *S Bahn* (elevated train in Berlin), and as such he was required to have an *Ahnenpas*. As it is written in the old German, Irene and I spent many hours translating to complete the following pages. Alas, there is still much information missing beyond the names and dates, and not much is known of my father's ancestry, with respect to the personal history of his ancestors, since he and his siblings were orphaned at a very early age.

—Dorothea

Note: Previous records were destroyed during World War I, probably during the time when Hindenberg defeated the Russians at Tannenberg, East Prussia. Spelling of last names have changed through the years. Old German spelling of names ending with either 'is' or 'in' indicates female.

DOROTHEA RUTH GUTZEIT

March 10, 1921 — June 30, 2005

Married twice

with

three children,

six grand children

&

ten great grand children*

* 2016

    Dorothea GUTZEIT was one of four sisters, however there were eight children living together in this family. Her father, from his previous marriage, brought two daughters into his second marriage. Then, on two separate occasions, when sisters of her mother died, Dorothea's mother brought these orphaned boy cousins to live in the family home. Dorothea was one of eight children raised in this household.

Auguste (Hertha) Anna Berta WEGNER
Jan 14, 1892- Sept 3, 1972

August Wilhelm Karl GUTZEIT
July 22, 1882- Oct 11, 1937

August had two daughters from his first marriage:

1. Hertha   *married*   Willy WAGENKNECHT 1903-1977
    Feb 18, 1908 - Aug 6, 1975
        Son: Winfried died age 30   *married*   Anneliese Kierein, one daughter: Sonja
        Son: Gerhardt   *married*   Doris Postma

2. Frieda.   *married*   Mr. MEIER
    1904 – 1974
       (step siblings)
       Daughter: Evelyne 1941- 2015   (son Oliver)…
       Daughter: Ingrid Gutzeit 1947   *married*   Heinz VOLTZ

Dorothea's mother and father had four daughters:

3. Dorothea Ruth — March 10, 1921 - June 30, 2005

4. Elizabeth (Lisa)   *married*   Heinz FLORIAN.
    Jan 3, 1923 -Feb 11, 2013   May 2, 1922- Nov 30, 2002
        Son: Matthias Aug 17, 1957-   (daughter Maike)…
        Son: Andreas Oct 13, 1958-   *married*   Cordula

5. Christa   *married*   Cecil George STEP (Calcutta)
    Oct 10, 1928 – 1983   Aug 23, 1926 – Oct 12, 2015
    (step siblings):
       Daughter: Karin Nov 10, 1956 - March 4, 2008
       Son: Martin Step Feb 5, 1951   *married*   Joyce
       (Salvadore)

6. Carin   *married*   Sigismund (Ziggi) BROCKMANN.
    Sept 16, 1935   Jun 22, 1928 –2012

    Dorothea's parents fostered two orphaned children from the mother's side. Cousins:

7. Gerd Lothar WEGNER   *married*   Gertrude
    June 7, 1929–Jan 1974   July 22, 1932
       Daughter: Barbel July 21, 1952
       Daughter: Martina Feb 8, 1956
       Daughter: Gabrielle July 20, 1960
       Son: Thomas May 8, 1964

8. Max-Walter JACOBEIT 1924 – 1924 (Max-Walter's mother Anna died during childbirth).
    He died while still a baby, of meningitis, soon after he came to live with the Gutzeit family.

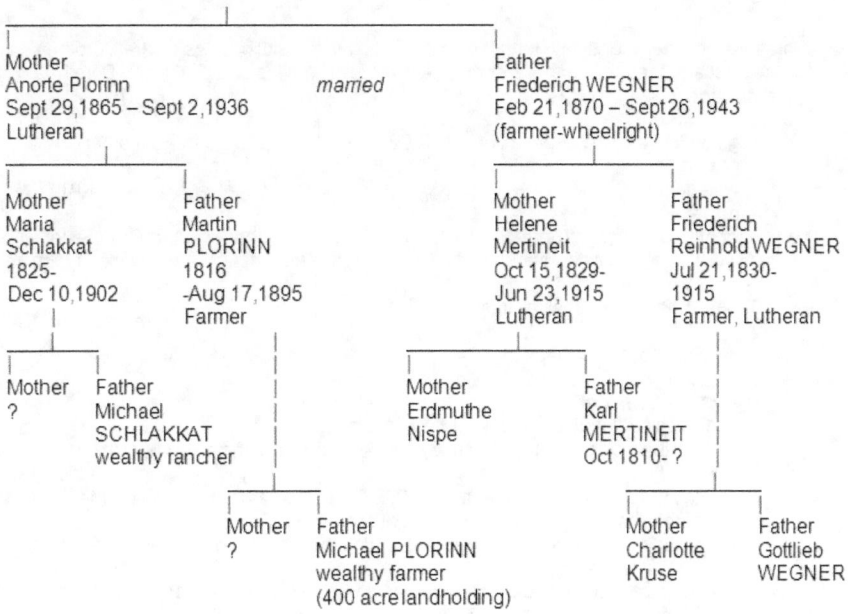

Dorothea's
MATERNAL ANCESTORS

Dorothea's Mother
Anna Auguste Berta (Hertha) Wegner
Jan 14, 1892 – Sept 3, 1972
Lutheran WWI nurse

Dorothea's Father: (see next page for Paternal)
August Wilhelm Karl Gutzeit
July 22, 1882 – Oct 11, 1937
Lutheran WWI cavalry officer, station master

Mother
Anorte Plorinn   *married*
Sept 29, 1865 – Sept 2, 1936
Lutheran

Father
Friederich WEGNER
Feb 21, 1870 – Sept 26, 1943
(farmer-wheelright)

Mother
Maria
Schlakkat
1825-
Dec 10, 1902

Father
Martin
PLORINN
1816
-Aug 17, 1895
Farmer

Mother
Helene
Mertineit
Oct 15, 1829-
Jun 23, 1915
Lutheran

Father
Friederich
Reinhold WEGNER
Jul 21, 1830-
1915
Farmer, Lutheran

Mother
?

Father
Michael
SCHLAKKAT
wealthy rancher

Mother
Erdmuthe
Nispe

Father
Karl
MERTINEIT
Oct 1810- ?

Mother
?

Father
Michael PLORINN
wealthy farmer
(400 acre landholding)

Mother
Charlotte
Kruse

Father
Gottlieb
WEGNER

Plorinn Ancestors came from East Prussia. Wegner Ancestors came from Austria. Information from marriage and birth certificates:

Records previous to these were lost or destroyed during the first World War.

Note: the land was in Lithuania but in the 18th century the land belonged to East Prussia.

MATERNAL ANCESTORS
Dorothea's Grandparents
and her mother's siblings

GRANDMOTHER: Anorte PLORINN
1865 – 1936

GRANDFATHER: Friederich WEGNER
1870 -1945

Dorothea's mother, Auguste (Hertha) was the oldest of ten siblings. Listed are Dorothea's mother first and then the mother's siblings — the aunts, uncles and cousins of Dorothea on the maternal side.

1. Auguste (Hertha) Anna Berta Jan 14, 1892 - Sept 3, 1972 (Dorothea's mother)

2. Amalie (Mali)   *married*   Max KALB
   Feb 14, 1894 - Feb 12, 1968
   Daughter: Annemarie (Born 1923) who became Sister Deborah, a Lutheran Sister with the
       Evangelical Sisterhood of Mary, originating in Darmstadt, Germany expanding to USA.

3. Bertha. 1886 she died as an infant

4. Anna. Sept 15, 1897- Dec 17, 1924   *married*   August JACOBEIT
   Son: Erwin (whereabouts and history unknown)
   Son: Max-Walter Dec 17, 1924 - 1924
       Anna died during childbirth at Max-Walter's birth
       (Dorothea's parents took the baby, however he died of meningitis within months)

5. Friederich (Fritz) Feb 2, 1900- Sept 23, 1972   *married*   Lina Daudert
   Son: Bernhard who died at the end of WWII at age 15.
       He had been taken by the Russians during the war and died when he returned
       from Russia seriously ill.
   Daughter: Imgard who died of starvation as an infant during the war
   Son: Walter who died in the 1970's
   Daughter: Gerda

6. Herman. Feb 29, 1902 – July 30, 1937   *married*   Gertrude Schmerbek
       Herman was a Nazi official, killed when he drove his car into a street car, while drunk.

7. Lina. Oct 1, 1904- Aug 14, 1969   *married*   Gustav GRAAP
   Son: Siegfried, a teacher in northern Germany, who had a daughter Corba.
   Son: Edwin, a police officer

8. Otto. Oct 13, 1906 - Sept 8, 1971   *married*   Anna Greken
       Otto was a building contractor who helped Dorothea's father build the family house in
       Berlin, Pinnauweg #4, Zehlendorf
   Son: Otto-Ernst
   Daughter: Rita

9. August (Walter). Nov 11, 1908 -197?   *not married*
       He was a tailor making precision military uniforms, specifically for submarine officers.
       He was living on submarines during WW II

10. Charlotte. Nov 20, 1911 - June 1929   *not married*
    Son: Gerd Jun 7, 1929 – Jan 1974
        Dorothea's parents raised the baby and he grew up as one of Dorothea's siblings.

MATERNAL ANCESTORS
Dorothea's great-grandparents,
and her grandmother's siblings

Maria Schlakkat.   *married*   Martin PLORINN
1825 – 1902   Mar 11, 1843   1816 – 1895

They had nine children. Although not the eldest, Anorte Plorinn is listed first and then her siblings. Not all dates are known.

1. Anorte Sept 29, 1865 – 1936 Lived and died in East Prussia, on the family farm. As a child Dorothea visited her grandmother on this farm every summer.

2. Martin (same name as his father) He went to America and became a farmer.

All other siblings *remained in East Prussia*

3. Daniel had four children, two sons Gustav and Fritz and twins who died at birth.

4. Michael had two sons and two daughters

5. Samuel had one son, also named Samuel and one daughter named Wilhelmina

6. August had three sons, Ferdinand, August and Willy

7. Christof married but did not have children

8. Whilemine married Mr. SCHILLOCK and they had four daughters:
   Whilemine (same name as mother),
   Justine
   Hertha (who was a twin, one died at birth).

   Note: Whilemine had a daughter Louise (Lisebeth) who was Dorothea's "aunt", who became close to Dorothea and her siblings, so they called her "Aunt Liesel". Louise had two children:
   a son who went to the USA
   a daughter Renate who went to Vancouver, Canada.

9. Erdmuthe married and had two daughters, Erika and Eva

MATERNAL ANCESTORS
Dorothea's grandparents,
and her great-grandparents,
grandfather's side

Friederich Reinholt WEGNER	married	Helene Mertineit
1830 - died before 1915		1829 - 1915

Four children:

1. Friederich (Dorothea's grandfather, her mother's father) was one of four siblings.

2. Ferdinand had several children and worked on an estate

3. August had several children and lived in Labiau, East Prussia

4. Ernst married and lived in Berlin

Note: since Friederich and Anorte had very few connections with the family on Friederich's side, not much is known about them. However a first cousin of Dorothea's grandfather was named Samuel. He went to Canada during the 1800's and was never heard of again. There is a grave in upper Canada Village, Ontario, marked Samuel Wegner; I wonder, could it be him?

MATERNAL ANCESTORS
Dorothea's great-grandfather

18th Century Ancestors of Friederich Reinholt Wegner.

I am now going back to my memory of what my mother and grandmother told me so long ago. The Wegner family came from Austria in the early 18th Century and moved to East Prussia. The family had become Protestants, and the Austrian Catholics did not tolerate them there. The motto of the Prussian King however was, "In my land everyone can become happy in their own religion, in their own way." The people who left their home land in Austria were well- educated journeymen, who brought with them the tools of their trade. They were welcomed in the sparsely populated land of East Prussia and were granted land to farm, as well as encouraged to keep up with their trades.

My grandfather was a wheel-right, making all sorts of wooden implements, wagons and wagon wheels. All through the generations, my ancestors valued education, freedom of religion and independence. East Prussia, since the time of the Middle Ages was a melting pot for people dissatisfied or persecuted for whatever reason. These settlers inter-married with the locals of Slavic background, as the many names of people and places indicate.

These first ancestors may have stayed in and around that particular region of East Prussia, but later generations dispersed. Men were drafted or volunteered to the military. As the family seems to have 'travel' in their genes, it seems that these military men would opt for service away from East Prussia. Also, often young women were sent to distant relatives to further their education, and new lives would be made. It is documented that ancestors of the Wegner branch of the family went to Russia, the United States, Sweden and Canada.

18th Century Ancestors of Maria Schlakkat.

There was a very large farm in Kirschnakeim, County Labiau, East Prussia. On March 11, 1843, my great-grandfather, Martin Plorinn, married the heiress of that farm, Maria Schlakkat. The farm, which had over 400 acres, was by European standards a very substantial farm. My great-grandfather served in the military with the Langen Kerls regiment in Potsdam, known as the Giants of Potsdam. One of the requirements of this regiment was height. Everyone had to be over six feet tall. This regiment, a hobby of the father of King Frederick the Great of Prussia, existed until the First World War.

Great-grandfather Martin Plorinn fought in the battle of Dueppler Schanzen in the Prussian war with Denmark in 1864. My great- grandfather had a younger brother, born late in the life of their parents, who also joined this Potsdam Giants regiment. The ruling Tsar of Russia, the last Tsar, requested that this brother come back to Russia. It was said that he became a very honored member of the Russian court. He must have been a remarkable man, for he was also later an honored citizen of Soviet Russia. When he died at the age of 103, some time in the 1950s, he was buried with full military honors. This honor bestowed by the Soviets, who ruled Russia once the Tsar fell, showed that my great-grandfather's brother was someone of worth, yet with no political hindrances.

Friedrich (Fritz) and Lina, my aunt and uncle (my mother's brother and his wife) received an invitation to the state funeral of their great-uncle. However, by the time the travel paperwork was completed, it was too late to attend. Although Fritz and Lina were living in the Russian zone of East Germany during the 1950s, there was simply too much paperwork for this trip to Moscow.

My great-grandfather, Martin Plorinn, while a soldier with that regiment, learned to drink in excess and in a short time, after his marriage to Maria, sold most of the land to support his drinking habit. By the time he was through selling, there was only enough left to purchase a four-acre piece of land in Lucknojen (later named Neuenrode, East Prussia). My grandmother Anorte Plorinn, one of Maria and Martin's children, later inherited this small piece of land.

My great-grandmother, Maria, was not only an heiress, but also beautiful woman who held herself straight and proud. Everyone treated her with great respect. But my mother told me that Maria often come to their home to hide when her husband came home drunk. Beyond this, there is little further information about Maria except that she spoke only Lithuanian.

This little four-acre piece of land, with a small house, was situated adjacent to the village green and the school in Gross Lucknojen (Great Lucknojen). In 1891, Maria's daughter, Anorte, married my grandfather, Friedrich Wegner and eight years later he sold that place and bought a parcel of land in Klein-Lucknojen which included six acres of meadow. This was home to my mother Auguste (Hertha) until she married my father August Gutzeit. My mother was only seven years old, in 1899, when she moved into that home but she remembered the renovations that her father did, and how all the villagers came to help. She would often talk about the large meals cooked for the many workers who helped build. But there was never any money exchanged. Everyone worked and helped for meals, and when the time came to help others with their big building projects, or farming tasks, it was for the meals, and for community.

Dorothea's PATERNAL ANCESTORS

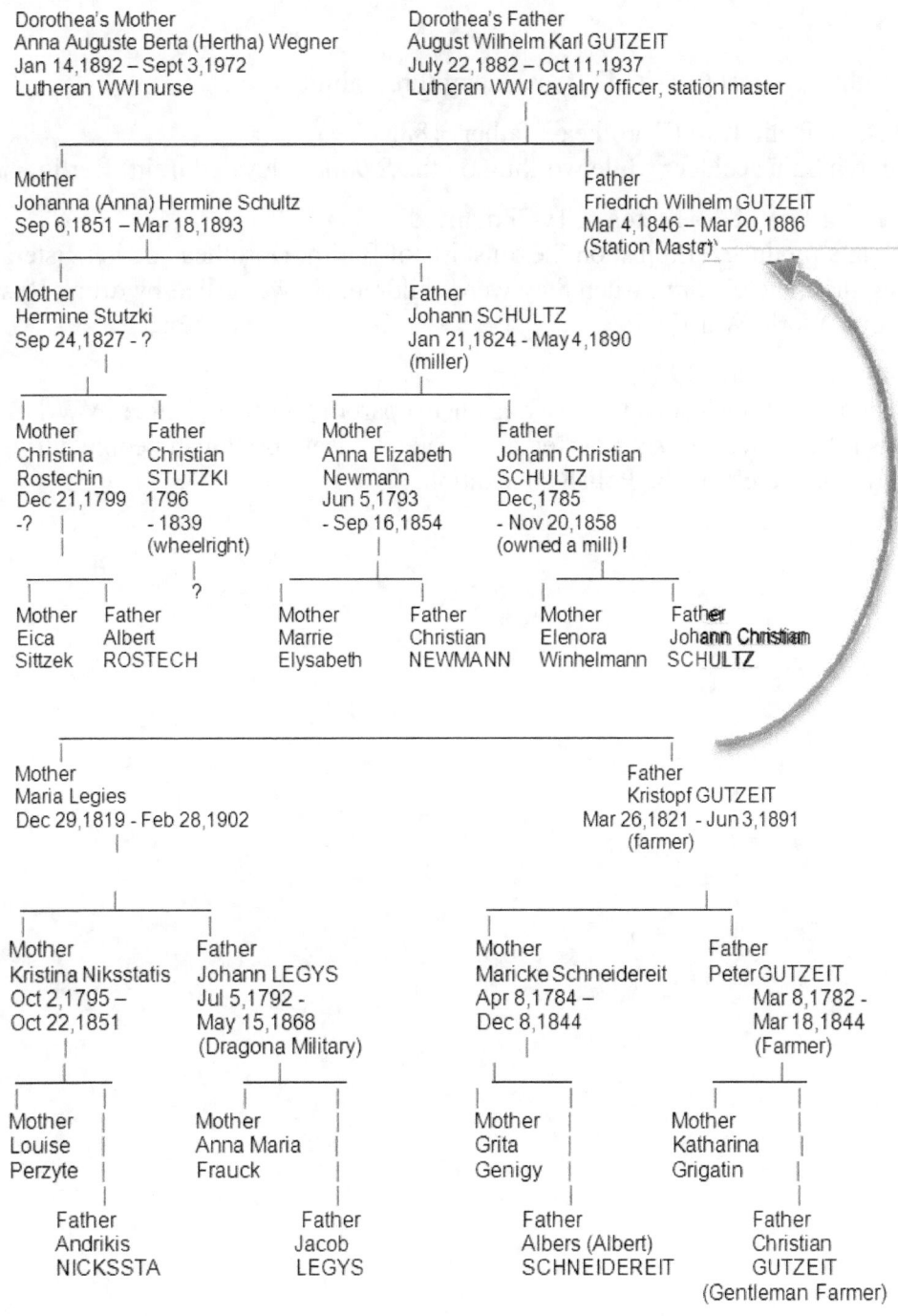

Dorothea's Mother
Anna Auguste Berta (Hertha) Wegner
Jan 14,1892 – Sept 3,1972
Lutheran WWI nurse

Dorothea's Father
August Wilhelm Karl GUTZEIT
July 22,1882 – Oct 11,1937
Lutheran WWI cavalry officer, station master

Mother
Johanna (Anna) Hermine Schultz
Sep 6,1851 – Mar 18,1893

Father
Friedrich Wilhelm GUTZEIT
Mar 4,1846 – Mar 20,1886
(Station Master)

Mother
Hermine Stutzki
Sep 24,1827 - ?

Father
Johann SCHULTZ
Jan 21,1824 - May 4,1890
(miller)

Mother
Christina
Rostechin
Dec 21,1799
-?

Father
Christian
STUTZKI
1796
- 1839
(wheelwright)

Mother
Anna Elizabeth
Newmann
Jun 5,1793
- Sep 16,1854

Father
Johann Christian
SCHULTZ
Dec,1785
- Nov 20,1858
(owned a mill) !

Mother
Eica
Sittzek

Father
Albert
ROSTECH

Mother
Marrie
Elysabeth

Father
Christian
NEWMANN

Mother
Elenora
Winhelmann

Father
Johann Christian
SCHULTZ

Mother
Maria Legies
Dec 29,1819 - Feb 28,1902

Father
Kristopf GUTZEIT
Mar 26,1821 - Jun 3,1891
(farmer)

Mother
Kristina Niksstatis
Oct 2,1795 –
Oct 22,1851

Father
Johann LEGYS
Jul 5,1792 -
May 15,1868
(Dragona Military)

Mother
Maricke Schneidereit
Apr 8,1784 –
Dec 8,1844

Father
Peter GUTZEIT
Mar 8,1782 -
Mar 18,1844
(Farmer)

Mother
Louise
Perzyte

Mother
Anna Maria
Frauck

Mother
Grita
Genigy

Mother
Katharina
Grigatin

Father
Andrikis
NICKSSTA

Father
Jacob
LEGYS

Father
Albers (Albert)
SCHNEIDEREIT

Father
Christian
GUTZEIT
(Gentleman Farmer)

PATERNAL ANCESTORS
Dorothea's father's siblings

Dorothea's father, August GUTZEIT, was one of three siblings:

1. August Wilhelm Karl (Dorothea's father) 1882 - 1937
   Killed in a train accident while working on the *S Bahn* (elevated train) Berlin, Germany

2. Ernst Aug 15, 1884 – March 4, 1945 married.
   Ernst ran a produce farm just on the outskirts of Berlin. Dorothea and her sisters remember visiting their uncle's farm when they were children. He was killed by drunk Russians soldiers, right after World War II

3. Johann 1880 – early 192?
   He lived in the Polish corridor that was once a part of Germany before WW I.
   He was killed when he was attacked and beaten to death by Polish people during a demonstration by Germans protesting the Polish annexation.

PATERNAL ANCESTORS

Not much is known of the Gutzeit side of the family as these three siblings, August, Ernst and Johann were orphaned at a very early age. August was only four years old when his father died, and barely eleven when his mother died in 1893. The mother was ill for a pro- longed period and died while having surgery in Koenigsberg (now Kaliningrad). The boys were left with and cared for by a girlfriend of the mother while she was ill, but when the mother died, the boys were all sent to different foster homes.

In later years when August was married (August and Hertha, Dorothea's parents) they went to visit this girlfriend of his mother's, in Goldap. At that time this girlfriend was 78 yeas old. An enterprising and busy woman, she was still taking in laundry for customers, but during that visit, there was no discussion of family history.

The foster father who raised August, (Dorothea's father) was a shoemaker, and highly qualified in his trade; he was commissioned to make custom riding boots for military cavalry officers.

There is little known about which area of Germany, (or Europe), the Gutzeits left when they moved to East Prussia, but they must have originated from elsewhere, as Gutzeit is not a Slavic name. It is safe to assume that these ancestors came to East Prussia seeking freedom of religion, as all the Gutzeits were Protestant Lutherans.

The Gutzeits later intermarried, as some of their names indicate.

Herbert STIMMING
1st husband of Dorothea

Very little information is available due to the war, politics and the destruction in Berlin, as well as the short marriage and early breakup, beyond what is written in Chapter Three of this book.

From past to most recent:

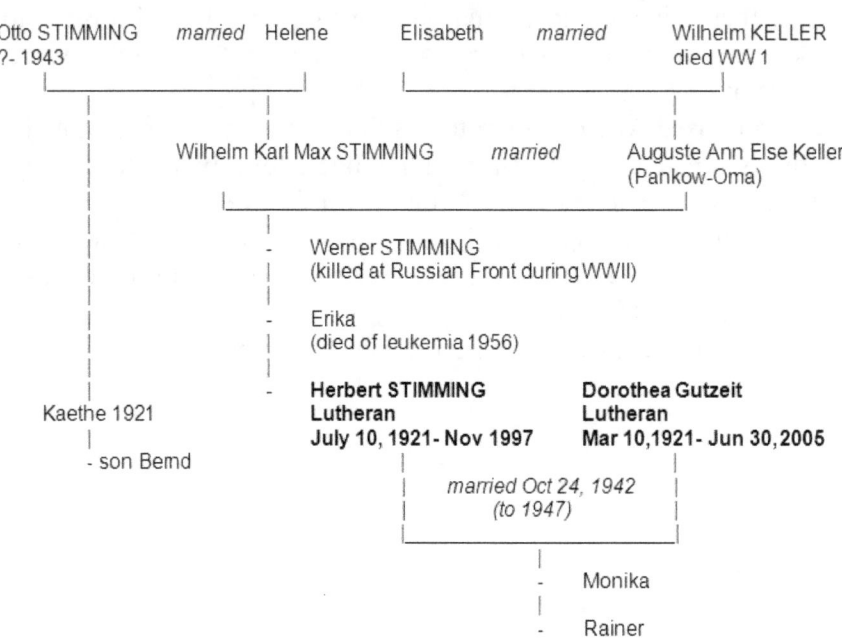

Otto STIMMING ?- 1943	*married*	Helene		Elisabeth	*married*	Wilhelm KELLER died WW 1

Wilhelm Karl Max STIMMING   *married*   Auguste Ann Else Keller (Pankow-Oma)

- Werner STIMMING (killed at Russian Front during WWII)

- Erika (died of leukemia 1956)

- **Herbert STIMMING**
  Lutheran
  July 10, 1921- Nov 1997

Dorothea Gutzeit
Lutheran
Mar 10,1921- Jun 30, 2005

married Oct 24, 1942
(to 1947)

Kaethe 1921

- son Bernd

- Monika

- Rainer

Josef Koenigsberger was an only child, raised by a single mom in pre-World-War-II Berlin Germany. He was born in Koenigshutte in Upper Silesia, which at the time of his birth was part of Germany, but was given to Poland as part of the World War I Peace Treaty.

Therefore, shortly after his birth in 1923, his parents decided to go back to Germany. Unfortunately this move was to cause the breakup of his parent's marriage. His father moved back to his birth place in central Germany, to the city of Neumarkt, and later remarried, while his mother took their six month-old baby, Josef, to live in Berlin, as she wanted to be near her sister Elli and her aunt Paula. Josef's status, as the only child, in that apartment complex where his mother and extended family lived, changed when his cousin Lydia was born in 1927. At this time Josef was almost six years old, but these two cousins became fast friends with Josef ever the protector, much to Lydia's frustrations, for no matter what she tried to do, Josef was forever correcting her, all the while hoping to guide her. But often his impatience got the better of him. However the close friend- ship, that developed as these two cousins grew up together through those turbulent years, continued throughout their lives, even through the distance of immigrating to two different countries.

Josef and Lydia lived in the apartment building, directly across from Potsdammer Platz and the fabled, pre-World-War-II, Haus Vaterland Hotel. During the second world war, when bombs fell like raindrops on Berlin Center, #46 Kothemer Strasse was destroyed. But #44, right next door, miraculously survived, and when Irene visited Berlin with Lydia in 2006, Lydia was able to describe and relive some of her childhood memories of that apartment building that Josef and his extended family called home.

You can still see the type of construction of this old five-story building, solid with huge entrances. Although renovated today, remnants of the original grey stone building with pink borders is still visible. The wooden carved door has been repaired and refurbished with new black iron handles and hinges. Lydia described how the ground floor of the apartment houses was occupied by little shops, a cigar store as well as others, and on the corner a brothel. The kids Josef and Lydia were not supposed to know about that, but they knew. Across the road, the huge Haus Vaterland complex housed live theatres, a music hall and many restaurants, each decorated with a theme from another country. The neighborhood was a busy place, with entertainment, noise and music and a never-ending source of amusement for the two kids as they perched on the two huge natural field-stone door stoppers in front of the house, and watched the rowdy lifestyle pass by on the road right in front of them! Lydia recalled the beer barrels being delivered by horse and carriage as they trotted down the street to Haus Vaterland. Josef, several years older, became both protector and tormentor. He was full of action, and was constantly urging the little girl to run faster, do better, when-ever they were building something or playing with the Josef's mechanical trucks or toys that he had received from his great-aunt Paula.

Between the houses was a gate and the cobblestone drive sloped down towards the street to allow the horse and carriages to enter to the back yard courtyard. This courtyard, enclosed by the houses, open to the sky above, completely paved with stones, became the children's playground. The stones on the courtyard floor, and were over the basements extending from the apartment houses. Placed sporadically between the stones were thick green glass bricks incorporated into the paving. This green glass provided the only light into the dark underground storage rooms.

Later as the children grew, Josef went to the Franciscan Catholic Jesuit School. A very disciplined environment for a young man who didn't enjoy book learning and craved the freedom of the outdoors and inventions. Lydia went to the *volkschule* or public school, and received a conventional education and went on to learn the trade of tailor and seamstress.

There is little information available of Josef's father and his paternal family as there was no contact between Josef's mother and his father. In fact even what she did know, she never shared with him, including telling him when his father eventually died. What information there is, came by way of a trip when Josef and Dorothea undertook to travel to Neumarkt, shortly after they were married, to see if they could find his father and family. This trip, was difficult as it was right after World War II, but it was important for Josef to find out what he could about his father's side. Sadly his father had passed by this time; However Josef was able to meet some of his step siblings and their children, and also his grandfather, who by this time was an old blind man. But even more sad, is that other than this visit and a few letters that stopped not long afterwards, there was no continuing contact fostered. We were able to collect names and some dates from a legal document that was mailed to Josef in 1957, to his new home in Canada. This document set out to explain the distribution of war damage reparation payments for his father, Johan Koenigsberger's property in Neumarkt that was bomb damaged, and these nominal funds were to be distributed to his children of which Josef was one

of five listed along with his step- siblings from his father's second marriage. Although his father was deceased at this time, his grand- father, Michael Koenigsberger, was still living, blind and cared for by Josef's step brother Georg, All siblings signed over this small inheritance to Georg.

The information available for Josef's mother, and the maternal side of his family, was collected from some information that Martha, Josef's mother was able to gather prior to 1944. There was much difficulty in obtaining information, as land of her ancestors kept shifting its political borders from Germany to Poland. After 1944, the task of obtaining records or any information was simply impossible, as it was either destroyed during the war, or not available due to the many political communication restrictions that resulted in what is known today as the 'cold war'.

Paula Gajowsky, Josef mother's aunt, never married. Early in her life she moved to Berlin and found work at Haus Vaterland where she became supervisor in charge of all the restrooms. When Martha took baby Josef and left her husband, it was to go to Berlin and stay with her aunt Paula, who helped Martha find work as seamstress, repair- ing uniforms, costumes and linens for Haus Vaterland. It was Aunt Paula who spoilt Josef, buying him all the big-ticket items such as his bike, and even his first kayak. Paula was a hard-working, enterprising woman, always resourceful even in the most difficult times.

During the last years of the war and right after, when Berlin fell leaving a starving and desperate people, she understood the situation, buying medical supplies in the west sector of Berlin and selling them at a profit in the east, where nothing was available. She became quite wealthy but of course all that stopped when the Berlin wall was erected, but she always managed.

Martha, Josef's mother, at the age of nine fell and dislocated her hip, leaving her with a limp for the rest of her life. In those days an injury of this type was not typically understood or treated. With her limp, her parents felt that she might never find a suitable husband, so she became the only one of the five children to receive a formal education and training. This helped her in later years as a single mom to raise Josef.

Martha was one of five siblings but throughout her life she remained close to only one, Ellie, who lived in Berlin in that same apartment house. But there is a tragic story that Lydia recalled about another sibling, August, Martha's brother. He had two children.

Ernst who died in WW II and also a daughter Erna, who drowned under suspicious circumstances in 1962. Erna married a charismatic but difficult man. They had a daughter and shortly after this baby's birth, he hypnotized his wife, Erna, and she marched into the water and drowned. Erna's father, August, was very distraught as he knew about this, and could do nothing about it. He left and went to Berlin. His wife, the baby's grandmother, stayed to take care of the baby, and said nothing for fear she might not be allowed to see the baby.

The husband, who did the hypnotizing, approached Lydia and asked her to sponsor him for immigration to the USA. Lydia said no.

Ellie married Arthur Nehls and they had one child, Lydia, who immigrated to the USA in 1947 when she married an American soldier (William Turner). Although Arthur would have liked to im- migrate to the USA, he was not allowed for he had belonged to the Communist party at some point before or during WW II.

Josef KOENIGSBERGER
2nd husband of Dorothea

Three children raised in that family home, two from Dorothea's first marriage, Monika and Rainer Stimming, and Irene, born to Dorothea and Josef shortly after their marriage.

From past to most recent:
MATERNAL ANCESTORS from Koenigshutte (now Poland)

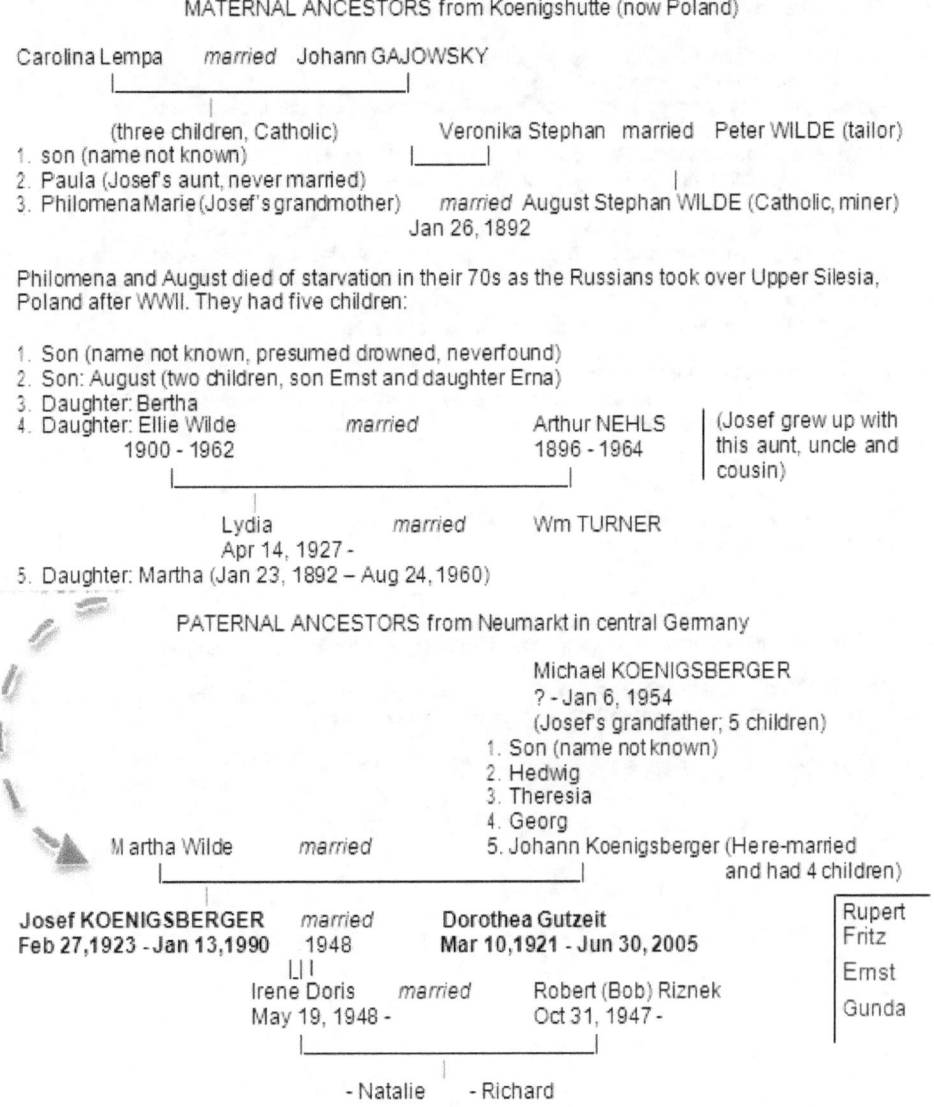

Carolina Lempa   *married*   Johann GAJOWSKY

(three children, Catholic)   Veronika Stephan   married   Peter WILDE (tailor)
1. son (name not known)
2. Paula (Josef's aunt, never married)
3. Philomena Marie (Josef's grandmother)   *married* August Stephan WILDE (Catholic, miner)
Jan 26, 1892

Philomena and August died of starvation in their 70s as the Russians took over Upper Silesia, Poland after WWII. They had five children:

1. Son (name not known, presumed drowned, never found)
2. Son: August (two children, son Ernst and daughter Erna)
3. Daughter: Bertha
4. Daughter: Ellie Wilde   *married*   Arthur NEHLS   (Josef grew up with
   1900 - 1962   1896 - 1964   this aunt, uncle and
                                                                           cousin)

Lydia   *married*   Wm TURNER
Apr 14, 1927 -
5. Daughter: Martha (Jan 23, 1892 – Aug 24, 1960)

PATERNAL ANCESTORS from Neumarkt in central Germany

Michael KOENIGSBERGER
? - Jan 6, 1954
(Josef's grandfather; 5 children)
1. Son (name not known)
2. Hedwig
3. Theresia
4. Georg
Martha Wilde   married   5. Johann Koenigsberger (He re-married
                                      and had 4 children)

Josef KOENIGSBERGER   *married*   Dorothea Gutzeit   Rupert
Feb 27, 1923 - Jan 13, 1990   1948   Mar 10, 1921 - Jun 30, 2005   Fritz
                                                                       Ernst
Irene Doris   *married*   Robert (Bob) Riznek   Gunda
May 19, 1948 -   Oct 31, 1947 -

- Natalie   - Richard

EULOGY

Obituary + Eulogy

Her Gift:

I wish to celebrate our Mother, Dorothea and her gift to us.

I wish to thank all of you for sharing in our loss and taking the time to comfort and remember.
We are not alone.
In fact, there are always people and life all around us,
Yet each of our lives is a private journey.
And at the end it is that celebration of a single life that is momentous.
For every life is singularly unique and precious.

As in many of her generation, my mother's life was formed and shaped not just by her parental expectations,
but also by historical circumstances and opportunities lost.
Ambitions remained unfulfilled and life was punctuated with disappointments and responsibilities.

With one giant leap she changed the course of her life and with it gave us,
her children, grandchildren and great-grandchildren, the greatest gift she could.

She left her home, her family, her work, her country and language; everything she knew
And together with her husband Joe, gave us the chance to be in an environment with opportunity to
Worship, work, grow and live in a peace and freedom still rarely matched in many other countries of the world today.
It is fitting that with her final journey she passed through Canada Day.

We are Canadians. But her gift did not come easy
Working hard and long, her exhausted body and poor health was a constant companion.
With diligence she learned and worked, in fact she pursued everything with the same intensity and expected nothing less from us.

She was a private person,
Who through her hardships and learning had formed many opinions,
Which she was always quick to share.

We would all have to agree that she was courageous and strong.
During the last fifteen years while she lived widowed and alone,
I had the privilege of coming to understand her and the frustrations that drove her many moods.

She knew life could be difficult and as is every mother's wish, she wanted happiness and success for all of us
She gave us a sense of independence and accountability. A blueprint to move forward.

I will miss you.

CONCLUSION

(Irene's note)

All is as it should be

There are no perfect relationships, and life is always full of circum- stance and difficulties. My mother, Dorothea, would have loved to spend her life reading books. Instead she found herself at the center of family life during a turbulent era, and then disappointments and the tragedy of war left her wondering how to raise two small children and if she could ever trust to love again. My father's enterprising and innovative ideas gave her a life that no book could have fulfilled.

My father, Josef, would have preferred to remain a free-spirited bachelor. Instead he embraced the responsibilities of family with genuine concern that each should grow and mature to be strong and able to face life's often unpredictable obstacles.

My grandmother, my mother's mother, Auguste (Hertha), was a determined woman and from what I remember from my childhood, not an easy person to feel close to. Her life was determined by the vow of service that she made during her youth, when frightened that a severe leg injury would require amputation. That vow was fulfilled as a WWI nurse, at a time when most women did not have professional careers; and when she found herself the caregiver of many children, not just her own, then caring for soldiers that came to her door during that second great war and always working to earn her keep with the garden. She had dreamed of love when her first love died, but found love with all she cared for. Her leg was amputated when she was in her mid-sixties, but not before she was given the chance to live and fulfill her vow.

1921 – 2005

A fascinating view of the "other side" in World War II, on the domestic front. Born in Berlin, Dorothea Gutzeit spent her formative years in Nazi Germany and in her war-torn city. She then forged a new life in Canada.

Thea with her father, 1934

"An amazing family story of courage and immigration."
— Siegfried Hansch (German-Canadian Business Association)

"An authentic and absorbing account of one woman's courage, tracing her life from early 20th century Germany to a new and challenging life in Canada, drawing on diaries, certificates and various documents, along with memories shared."
— H. Zobl (Professor Emeritus, Carleton University)

Daughter Irene Riznek (Koenigsberger) was born in Germany and came to Canada as a child. She prepared this autobiography based on historical certificates, documents and *Annenpas* records, and on her mother's notes and their many conversations. She has a son and a daughter, and lives in Ontario.

Cover photo: Dorothea age 21, Berlin, 1943

ISBN 978-1-927032-49-7
90000
9 781927 032497

Petra Books

Autobiography
petrabooks.ca
978-1-927032-49-7 print
978-1-927032-50-3 digital